NOT HERE TO BE
Served

Memoirs of a Peace Officer

Sheriff Alfonzo Williams

Edited by Ty Hager

Copyright 2020 Alfonzo Williams

Sheriffalfonzo.com

Front cover photo by Mark Brookes

Rear cover photo by Heather Ivey Bryant

Table of Contents

EDITOR'S NOTE 2

INTRODUCTION 3

CHAPTER ONE: KEYSVILLE 6

CHAPTER TWO: Mansion in the Projects 13

CHAPTER THREE: Potato Log Gets a Job 20

CHAPTER FOUR: New Wheels, New Home 25

CHAPTER FIVE: Augusta PD Badge #287 30

CHAPTER SIX: Aiming to Succeed 38

CHAPTER SEVEN: Fatherhood and Finances 42

CHAPTER EIGHT: The Academy 48

CHAPTER NINE: Field Training Officer Williams 52

CHAPTER TEN: Making Detective 62

CHAPTER ELEVEN: The Mary Colley Stewart Case 71

CHAPTER TWELVE: The Mad Mayor and Holy Matrimony 79

CHAPTER THIRTEEN: Broken Promises 84

CHAPTER FOURTEEN: Stepping Back and Stepping Up 90

CHAPTER FIFTEEN: The Saddest Day 96

CHAPTER SIXTEEN: A New Daughter and a Crazy Boss 101

CHAPTER SEVENTEEN: To the DA and Back 107

CHAPTER EIGHTEEN: Hometown Chief 115

CHAPTER NINETEEN: Getting Ready to Run 123

CHAPTER TWENTY: Politicking 126

CHAPTER TWENTY-ONE: Working the Dream 133

ACKOWLEDGEMENTS 141

SHERIFF ALFONZO'S POUND CAKE RECIPE 143

Dedication

This book is dedicated to my mother, my wife, and my daughters.

Without you and my faith I would be nothing...

EDITOR'S NOTE

Almost every word you're about to read is Sheriff Alfonzo Williams'. My role was simply to put them all in order, based on our many hours of recorded phone conversations and hundreds of pages of notes from our transcribed chats and historical records.

The goal of every writer is to tell a good story. If, along the way, lessons are learned or insights gained, well, that's just icing on the pound cake (you'll appreciate that reference later).

Not Here to be Served has been an amazing journey *about* the amazing journey of probably one of the most honest and genuine people I've had the great pleasure to call a friend.

Ty Hager, May 2020

INTRODUCTION

More than anything, it's about service and gratitude.

It may sound disingenuous, but those who really know me know better. Those are the reasons I chose work over socializing through my school years, those are the reasons I went into law enforcement right out of high school, those are the reasons for pretty much *everything* I've done – or tried to do – throughout my life.

Those are the reasons I'm writing this book.

Plus, Oprah got me fired up.

I'd been wanting to tell my story for some years – had received encouragement from friends and family, many of whom told me to *just start writing*. I hadn't. It's kind of a big job when you think about it: I've been around for going on half a century, and in law enforcement now for over thirty of those years. I've faced trials and hardship and adversity, just like anyone who's been around a while, but – of course – have a story that is all my own.

Well, *lots* of stories.

The vast majority of our families' histories are *oral histories*. That's the way it's always been, I guess. But oral histories tend to become distorted over time. I'm sure you've heard of – or even *played* - that game where you whisper something to the person next to you, then they whisper it to the person next to *them*, and it just goes down the line. By the time it gets to the *last* person in line, it usually bears little resemblance to what you *originally* whispered. I think that's what oral histories are like.

I wanted to write my story down but kept putting it off. Like I said BIG job.

Then I went to New York City to see Oprah Winfrey on her "2020 Wellness Tour." Oprah's been firing people up for longer than I've been in law enforcement, and this tour was all about getting yourself together, about doing what you want at this stage in life. About *accomplishing* something.

I started working on this book the next day. Thanks, Oprah!

There are many who would say I've *already* accomplished a lot. I was brought up in the most abject poverty one could imagine - one of seven kids raised by a single African American mother in the Deep South – and managed to work and persevere through it, to reach what for me is the pinnacle of success in my chosen field: I was elected sheriff of Burke County, Georgia – my home – in 2016.

There are also those who would say that writing a book is an "ego" thing. Again, those who say that just don't *know* me.

Then there are those who would question exactly *how* writing a book furthers my stated cause of "service and gratitude." Which reminds me of two of my favorite quotes – both of which serve and guide me to this very day.

The first comes from Scripture: "The Son of Man came not to be served, but to serve and to give his life as a ransom for many." I'm by no means what you'd call a "Bible-thumper," but my faith is very important to me, and I believe we are *all* the Sons and Daughters of

Man. I think it's an *obligation* to serve Mankind. I also think that if we're going to change society, we have to do it through knowledge and education. And that sometimes we have to do it one-by-one. If my story helps *a single person* to find hope or inspiration, then I will have served.

The second quote comes from my mother Rosa Lee Williams, whom I admire and respect more than words can say. We didn't have much growing up, but we always had love and we always had a meal. Of course, kids often don't understand just how valuable that is, and we were sometimes prone to grumbling about our hardships – about the things we *didn't* have. And Momma always told us that if we didn't appreciate what we had, we didn't have to look very far to find folks who had it worse. And *that*, she said, was "enough to say Grace over."

My story may not change thousands of lives. It may not change hundreds, or even dozens. But it may change *one*.

And that's enough to say Grace over.

CHAPTER ONE
KEYSVILLE

Up until the first grade, I had to go to the bathroom in a bucket.

I've seen a lot of poverty in my time – both while living in it and, second-hand, as a law-enforcement officer – but going-in-a-bucket poverty is about as low down the economic-status food chain as you can get. It was my job to empty the bucket every morning. That was as crappy (and unpaid at that) a job as I've ever had. Fortunately, we all did our business outdoors as much as possible, using a garden hoe to dig a hole in a rear secluded area of the side or back yard, then using leaves or newspaper or even brown grocery bags (I distinctly recall rubbing the bags together to smooth the rough texture) for toilet paper before covering it up.

All that remains of our home in Keysville

There were nine of us living in that ramshackle three-bedroom wooden-frame house, which sat supported on piles of rocks and small boulders off a dirt road in rural Keysville, Georgia (in Burke County on the South Carolina border – Waynesboro is the county seat and the nearest

Our mother's Aunt Bertha, relaxing in the off-limits-to-kids living room in Keysville.

"town," but most of us were born in the hospital in Augusta). In one bedroom I shared a bed with my grandfather Lucious. My twin brother Alonzo and older brother Homer shared a bed, and my older sister Angela and younger sister Jennifer shared a rollaway, all in that same room. My great-aunt (my mother's mother's sister, she was "Aunt Vene" to us) had a bedroom to herself. Momma and my two youngest sisters Cassandra and Teresa shared the third (this was the bedroom that had a TV – I have faded memories of watching *The Young and the Restless* with Momma and some of the siblings). The house also had a kitchen and a small sitting room, but the latter was off-limits to anyone but grown-ups and our frequent grown-up guests.

Of course, us kids were all little and had nothing much to compare our conditions to, so we didn't really know how rough we had it. We didn't know that there was excitement to be had beyond playing across the road in an old junk pile (used to burn trash) or getting the occasional truckers – going

Me on my Aunt Vene's lap

past our house to and from a nearby logging site – to blow their horns. We didn't know that most people in America didn't run a hose from a well to fill a #3 metal washtub for bathing, or to fill a rickety old washing machine (which sat outside) to do laundry. We didn't think it unusual to be grateful for the body heat of our bedmates as the winter wind whipped up through gaps in the rotted wooden floor slats on those nights when the fireplace and the quilts and blankets didn't quite do the trick. We were kids. This was our normal. To us, our uncle Lucious (son of the grandfather I bunked with) – who lived a brisk walking distance up the road in the opposite direction of my Aunt Lula's trailer – epitomized "living in luxury." He had a brick house and running water.

Our Grandaddy Lucious

Although us seven kids didn't all have the same fathers, our mother never allowed a man to spend the night. The closest we had to a "father figure" – apart from our oldest brother Homer, who would grow into the role - was Mathis Abrams (father to Cassandra and Teresa), who was also one of the first to teach me about service and gratitude. He went by the nickname "Pet," and was one of the kindest and most honorable men I've ever known. He never treated the rest of us any differently than his own biological children – he never gave them more than he gave *us*. We loved the Friday night trips to the store to get candy, loved when he brought us meals from the local "Li'l Chick," loved those nights when our mother would make his favorite dinner of mac and cheese with biscuits and smoked sausages, and loved when he brought us ice cream and watermelon – delicacies for *any* kid. He drove a beige Ford pickup with something loose in one wheel, so we knew when he was coming down the road, and he always had an excited, giggling welcoming committee.

Apart from the pickup, Pet liked nice cars (especially Buicks – I remember a brown one, then a blue one). We heard he always paid cash, and always bought them new, because he said he didn't want to buy a car someone else had farted in.

He always said a child who was misbehaving needed wood and water. "Wood on the butt and water in the eyes." He had a hearty laugh, and said he wanted to be buried on his stomach so he could tell the world to kiss his butt.

Pet was our anchor and got us through many times when we otherwise would have gone without. Clothes, shoes, and other basic necessities were fruits of Pet's kindness and generosity, often provided via a Sears credit card he gave my mother. He was an inspiration and a friend. Many years later, after he was prescribed a medication which caused his kidneys to fail, I would sit with him at the old Talmadge hospital in Augusta as he got the dialysis to keep him going until he could get a transplant. It was the least I could do. Pet was as proud of me becoming a police officer as he would have been of his own son. I miss him and wish he could see me now.

I didn't really know my own father, although I saw him almost every day. He lived next door to my Uncle Lucious and was – like our uncle, a school bus driver. Whether out of fear or respect, we kept our distances. That was confusing to a young boy of course, and I grew up wondering often what was wrong with me, why did this man have relationships with some of his children but not with me? I was too young to understand that there was a difference between legitimate and illegitimate in that context. I never really held a grudge, though. My twin brother Alonzo wasn't as forgiving, and harbored resentment for years. Our father is still alive – he's eighty-six and in a nursing home, suffering from dementia, but can still dance like John Travolta and especially loves the Electric Slide.

Our mother worked full-time as the Assistant Foods Supervisor at nearby Boggs Academy (about the only thing for which Keysville is particularly known, BA was a Presbyterian school founded in 1906 by Freedmen) until '74, when she had to quit to take care of Aunt Vene and Granddaddy. Us kids mostly stayed out of trouble, but kids will be kids, and one of my misadventures landed me in the Burke County hospital.

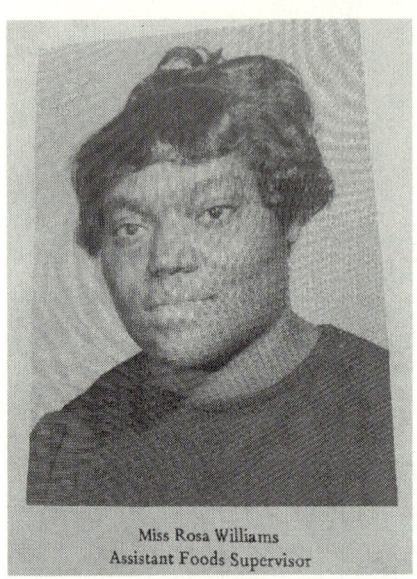

Miss Rosa Williams
Assistant Foods Supervisor

From the Boggs Academy Yearbook

Alonzo and I were playing around with an old, discarded washing machine which sat on the porch. We'd messed around with it before (kids will, after all, create fun wherever they find it) but, apparently, we hadn't messed with it since before the bees built a hive inside. There *is* no good age to go the emergency room for head-to-toe bee stings, but when it happens early you have more of your life left to remain terrified of

Boggs Academy

bees.

I wasn't much older than that when snakes got added to the list of things I wanted absolutely nothing to do with. Playing in a rimless tire, as carefree as a boy in the summertime can be, suddenly scarred for life by the black snake which slithered from the darkness inside the tire, so that it seemed at first like part of the tire had come alive. I'd have to say that I jumped out of that tire more quickly than the snake, but it was close.

I still have an unhealthy fear of both bees and snakes, and don't care for fishing or hunting or *any* outdoor work or pastime which might bring us in close proximity. Fortunately, law enforcement requires very little in the way of bee-keeping or snake handling, or I'd probably be doing something else.

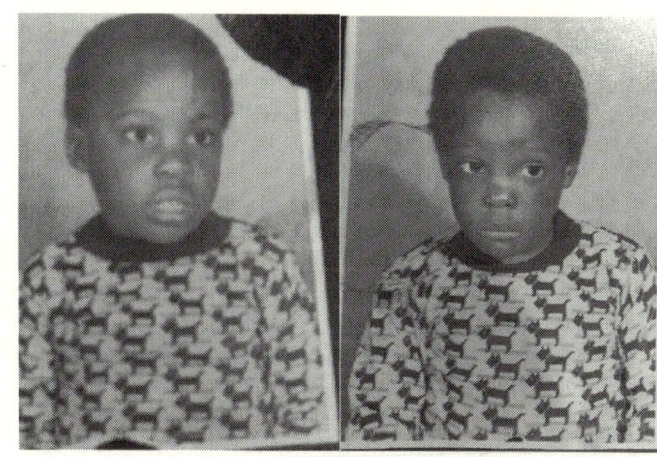

My twin brother Alonzo (L) and I, wearing matching shirts

Now that I think about it - considering my history - I probably would have overcome both those fears if I'd had to. I'd probably be teaching bee-keeping and snake handling. But I'm really glad it hasn't come to that.

Faith was always – and still is – important to us. We went to church every Sunday, alternating between our own (which only met the second Sunday of each month) and the Walker Grove Baptist Church – also within walking distance.

We didn't have much during those earliest years of my childhood, but we had lots of love and plenty to eat and plenty of friends. Enough to say Grace over.

I had just completed the first grade at Palmer Elementary in Keysville when Momma gave us the news that we would soon have even more to say Grace over: like the theme song to the sitcom *The Jeffersons* (which I hadn't actually seen yet), we were "Movin' on up."

We were headed to the projects.

CHAPTER TWO

Mansion in the Projects

Waynesboro, Georgia is the seat of Burke County - one of the original eight counties (and the second largest in square miles) in what was the southernmost of the original thirteen U.S. colonies. Named after the Revolutionary War hero General Anthony Wayne (known as "Mad Anthony"), the town actually has one of those "George Washington Slept Here" monuments, sitting on Liberty Street in front of the Golden Pantry. Waynesboro is also known as *The Bird Dog Capital of the World*, which explains the pointing dog on the water tower.

It really isn't much different from any small town in the Deep South: lots of farms (corn, peanut, and dairy farms mainly), church on Wednesdays and Sundays, high school football on Friday nights during the fall. Also like many Southern towns, the railroad tracks divided the Blacks from the Whites, as did – up until nearly the mid-eighties – separate drinking fountains in the old County Courthouse.

Us kids didn't care anything about any of that in the summer of 1978 – we were in a five-bedroom house with two bathrooms, running water and central heat! Compared to the shack in which we'd spent our lives up until then, our home at 536 Pilgrim Way was a mansion!

And we had my twin brother Alonzo's asthma and our family physician Dr. Charles Green's kindness to thank. Dr. Green had been telling Momma for some time that we needed to move into town to be nearer the hospital – some of my brother's attacks could be pretty severe - and he helped us get into government housing. Another example of "service" (and going above and beyond the call of duty) which inspired me from an early age.

Pilgrim Way was still a long way from *Easy Street*, and every new chapter marks the end of another. Our Aunt Vene had passed not long before the move, and our granddaddy (who'd had a toe - then a leg - amputated) was beginning his own final chapter. Momma still stayed home and took care of him full-time, and we all did what we could to help make it easier.

As much as we loved our new place, the move from rural to urban was a bit of an adjustment. Our neighbors were no longer *related* to us we were surrounded by strangers. Until the Haynes moved in.

We had been in our new home for a few months when - one Saturday morning - a large and loud two-ton rusted truck pulled up in the cul-de-sac. It caught our attention because it was full of furniture. And people. One by one, nine children of various ages (two boys and seven girls) and an adult woman got out of the truck. The kids looked like country kids, wearing hand-me-down clothes, with unkept hair and bare feet.

They too were being raised by a single mother, Viola Haynes, who was doing the best she could to provide for her family after the accidental death of their father. We and the Haynes kids had a lot in common: All of us were on public assistance and had mothers who instilled discipline and respect. All of us were looking to make new friends. We became very fond of the Haynes family and remain so today.

When school started that fall, we all waited together every morning for the #65 bus to Waynesboro Elementary. I'll never forget that old yellow bus – packed standing-room-only (including the kids in the stairwell), always either too hot or too cold, with that mildewy smell that comes from seats rained on one too many times through left-open windows, the sounds of a multitude of excited conversations intermingling with the grinding of not-quite-meshed gears.

I didn't love school, but I didn't hate it either. I wasn't a *great* student, but nor was I a poor one. According to those tests we had to take – filling in multiple-choice answers with a #2 pencil – I was on the lower end of the academic scale, but I think what I learned about *people* more than made up for my shortcomings in reading, writing, and arithmetic. I just learned enough about *those* things to get me through.

What I remember most about Waynesboro Elementary – like what I remember most about *most* of my childhood – are the people who set examples and became inspirations. Teachers like Trudie Brown and Carolyn Hamilton – both strict disciplinarians (Mrs. Hamilton would give anyone who misbehaved thirteen whacks with a paddle – I don't know why it had to be *thirteen*, but it was *definitely* an unlucky number) who also showed through words and deeds that they truly *cared*, that their careers weren't just jobs but *callings*.

Mrs. Brown was a brown-skinned older lady who taught fourth grade and kept us kids in line (particularly during class change, when teachers were required to stand at their respective doorways and act as shepherds of our rowdy flock) with a yardstick and a firm "Don't ask me anything. Don't tell me anything. *I'll* tell you what you need to know." And she did.

She also took a liking to me (although I was by no means spared the occasional popping with her yardstick), and often sent me to fetch school papers or other forgotten items from her house, which bordered the school.

Mrs. Brown (who later became Mrs. Brown Gordon) and her husband were murdered here in Burke County in 2010 by a former student looking for odd jobs. I was teaching Law Enforcement at Augusta Technical College at the time and had just – a week earlier – run into the

Trudie & Ralph Gordon

elderly couple at the grocery store (I'd promised to bake them a pound cake soon). That same week I'd also run into their killer at the Pancake House where he worked (I was there with a group of students, who'd commented on the man's odd behavior). The coincidences and tragedies in life are sometimes unreal. Life *itself* is as real as it gets.

Life in the projects was pretty real too: sometimes real sad, sometimes real inspirational, oftentimes that inspiring combination of both, when hard times bring out the best in people and serve as life-long examples. A lot of lemonade was made from those lemons, thanks to folks like Susan Coursey – then Director of the Department of Family and Children's Services – who would occasionally give our mother extra food stamps to tide us over. Back in those days, food stamps came in little books. While there were families in the projects who were a bit more cavalier with their monthly allotment (it wasn't unusual to see our friends given food stamps by their parents to use how they pleased), Momma was *much* stricter – she treated those food stamps like real money, and never wasted them on such luxuries as candy and junk food. Mrs. Coursey knew this and understood that sometimes the help we received wasn't enough to feed eight mouths for a month.

All of us on the front porch at Pilgrim Way

Bessie and Willie McCloud were other great examples and inspirations. They were educators in the public-school system – she a counselor, he a science teacher – and we thought they were *rich*! They had a beautiful brick home with hardwood floors, a fireplace, and an immaculately-kept yard. As we got older, the McCloud's kept my sisters and I employed – me maintaining the lawn, my sisters cleaning the house. Over the years, they provided me with more work – cleaning their church (Westminster Presbyterian) once a week - and even helped out with college expenses for my sisters. Just amazing people and amazing examples for us kids.

Through the McClouds, we met the Stones. Samuel and Leila - also both educators – hired us for odd-jobs as well and provided help when we needed it most.

Of course, being kids, we weren't always *receptive* to some of the opportunities availed us: I'll never forget the Reverend Gordon Quaye driving around the neighborhood, gathering up young black boys to give us golf lessons. We'd hide. We didn't understand the value of mentoring or the benefits of a positive black male role model – we just knew it was too hot to chase around a little white ball. Our mother, however, knew better. So we went golfing with Reverend Quaye. His wife Viola (who was Willie McCloud's sister) later hired me to work in their home after the Reverend became ill and – shortly thereafter – died. I regularly played bingo with Viola at a nursing home here (as part of the sheriff's office Community Outreach program), until her recent passing.

My childhood memories are full of those who – beginning with my mother – inspired and encouraged me. But I'll never forget the pound cakes.

Momma was a great cook, and her way of offering comfort and solace during trying times was to bake a pound cake. Whether it was a neighbor who'd lost a family member or a church friend (we were members of the Forest Hill Baptist Church, but our mother made sure we went to services at churches of different denominations – including Church of Christ or Jehovah's Witness) who was going through hard times, our mother would bake them a pound cake. It was her way of being of service.

And, from an early age, I knew *I* wanted to be of service too.

Living in the projects, we had our fair share of contact with the police most often they were in the neighborhood to take care of a domestic disturbance, and we'd usually watch them through our front window, as most domestic disturbances happened after our curfew (which was the moment the street lamp on the corner came on).

Sometimes the police were there for crimes much more severe: Our neighbors' daughter Daisy Jones was stabbed by a friend of hers named Lisa Preston. Our oldest brother Homer dated Daisy's sister Glenn, and I remember them as a close family who often invited me to dinners of rice and gravy and red Kool Aid. The Joneses lived two doors down from us and - at some point after she'd been stabbed - Daisy left a trail of blood on the sidewalk in front of our house. I remember Momma cleaning the stain with a broom, hot water, and Comet.

Sadly, many young black men from the projects grow up thinking of law enforcement as "the enemy" (there was a guy in our neighborhood named "Freight Train," who was known for beating police officers up). Not me. I was just eight years old when I decided it was my destiny not just to serve, but *"To Protect and Serve."*

But that was quite a few hard years away. In the meantime, I learned to bake pound cakes.

CHAPTER THREE
Potato Log Gets a Job

When I was fourteen or fifteen years old, I stole a baseball mitt and felt so sick and guilty I crapped my pants. I've never been able to say for certain that one was related to the other, but I haven't stolen anything since. I don't think I've crapped my pants since that day either (or if I have, it's not been out of guilt from stealing).

This happened during my first trip to Atlanta – the Waynesboro Optimist Club (many of my early role models and inspirations were members) had sponsored a trip to see a Braves game for a group of disadvantaged youth. I committed my theft during the game and got my punishment on the way home – a punishment which continued over the next few years, every time I was made fun of for soiling myself.

I was no stranger to taunting: In addition to being called "dumb" for being held back in the seventh grade (the only one of us kids to suffer such shame – I was *amazed* my mother didn't give me a beating for that), I was a husky kid, and for years had been called "fat boy" or "potato log" by my classmates. The latter nickname was due to my fondness for the fried potato wedges sold at Delmac, the convenience store down the road. They were three for a quarter, bought with money from selling glass Coke bottles for a dime each. Most of the kids bought candy I wanted those potato logs with ketchup and hot sauce! Of course, the kids attributed my weight to that - hence the nickname. Kids can be cruel in creative ways sometimes.

I probably would have been much more hurt by the names if I'd socialized more, but I didn't have time for that - I was always *working*!

Our mother instilled a very strong work ethic in all of us. For as long as I can remember, we worked. On weekdays, Momma called roll twice a day, either to get us off to school or assign chores.

This is an article from the Waynesboro *True Citizen* from 2013 about our family

Us older siblings took turns making the family breakfast. Saturdays were for ironing Momma's work uniforms (she was very particular about the crease), raking the yard and washing walls, or washing oil stains off the cul-de-sac parking spaces (and we didn't even own a *car*) and cleaning the city polycart (garbage bin). As I got older, in addition to the various odd jobs given me by neighbors and friends, I sold newspapers and worked summers in the fields for Ted Sasser (he'd send a pickup truck into the projects looking for kids to pick peas or peaches or corn – my desire for money was greater than my fear of snakes and bees). Each year at Exchange Club Fair-time, I and other kids would flock to the fairgrounds, hanging around and bugging the carnies until someone put us to work. As much as I dreamed of being a policeman, in those days I also dreamed of being old enough to just get *any* kind of real job – one with regular hours and a regular paycheck.

One big misconception about government-assisted housing – or at least as it existed in Waynesboro at the time – is that it's a free ride. It's not. Our rent was based on our household income, which meant that each additional paycheck meant additional rent. Kind of seems like incentive to *not* work, and for some I guess it was.

Not for us. After all, even with the higher rent, it was still more *money*. It was a chance to save to buy a car, or even just buy a pair of shoes from somewhere other than the Dollar Store. A regular job with a regular paycheck was instilled in us as the *only* way to get ahead.

And so, at fifteen, I became a bag boy at the Piggly Wiggly. The Waynesboro Piggly Wiggly was just under a three-mile walk from the house, and I walked round-trip *twice* the day I got my first real job. The first time was to talk to Mr. Lee, the manager. I remember him standing near the produce section of the store, looking over my application, and saying, "Well, you're a strong guy and you're eager to work and I'm going to give you a chance." I told him I had a twin brother who was *also* a strong guy and eager to work, and that we needed to make money "'cause we got rent to pay."

So I ran home and got Alonzo, and we *both* got jobs that day.

During my year and a half at Piggly Wiggly I went from bag boy to office clerk to front-end manager, helped open up a brand new store, and was probably known as much as "that guy who's going to be a Piggly Wiggly manager" as "that guy who wants to be a cop."

My career at Piggly Wiggly (along with any notion that I might choose a career path other than law enforcement) came to an abrupt end when Dennis Brooks, the manager at the new store, disrespected a co-worker. I felt the need to stand up for him.

"Mr. Brooks," I said, "I don't like the way you talked to (whatever the kid's name was)."

"Well, if you don't like it, Alfonzo, you can leave," he told me.

So I did.

I was pretty proud of myself that day. I'd stood up for an underdog, put myself on the line, and accepted the consequences.

Momma wasn't so proud. Later that night, I found her sitting alone in the living room, crying her eyes out. I hadn't realized that we were just *barely* making ends meet, or what a blow to the family finances my noble resignation was. I knew that between my brother and I we were bringing home more than our mother was from her cafeteria job at Blakeney Elementary School (she'd started there in '85), but – in my pride and misdirected sense of virtue – hadn't considered the real consequences.

There's really very little worse than making your mother cry – at least not to me. I was as ashamed of *that* as I was about the baseball mitt. Except, rather than soiling myself, I went out and got another job.

Thank God I had a car!

Momma at the kitchen table

CHAPTER FOUR

New Wheels, New Home

Some of my favorite childhood memories are of frequent weekend road trips to Augusta with my Aunt Lula – early on in a green two-door Gran Torino, later in a brown *four-door* Gran Torino. Every weekend trip would include a stop at Church's Fried Chicken. Aunt Lula would get us chicken and rolls with a couple of drinks to share among us – always to go – and we'd pull over to the side of the road to enjoy our treat. Aunt Lula and our mother were very close, and her child Pat and Pat's children Brandon, Valencia, and Jazzlyn were much more like siblings than first- and second-cousins. Those were happy times to me!

Our mother never learned to drive, so Aunt Lula was pretty much the "wheels" of the family during our time at the shack in Keysville and – to a lesser extent – once we moved into the projects. Mainly, though, we walked.

In front of Aunt Lula's Gran Torino

Except for to and from school, we walked *everywhere*: the Piggly Wiggly, the Delmac convenience store a quarter-mile away, Sears and Dr. Green's (each two miles), or just to see friends or play some ball. It wasn't unusual at all to make *several* trips a day back and forth to one place or the other, so I imagine there were days I walked ten miles. If it was within walking distance, we walked. If it wasn't...well, we just rarely went those places. Or Aunt Lula drove us.

So it was a pretty big moment in our family's life when – not long after my sixteenth birthday – my Uncle Lucious, Jr. took me and my hard-saved Piggly Wiggly earnings to Rick Stewart at Stewart Chevrolet, where – with a little help from First National Bank of Waynesboro - I bought an Oldsmobile 98 Regency. It was a big four-door that looked like something an old man would drive, but it was clean and it was *mine*.

It really came in handy after I quit my Piggly Wiggly job.

Until I was sixteen, I'd never been to a McDonald's. I hadn't even known what "the Golden Arches" *meant*. After I realized what a bind I'd put our family in by quitting Piggly Wiggly, I got a job there. It was a thirty-mile drive each way to the McDonald's in Augusta, so my net income was less than what I'd been making at Piggly Wiggly, but I learned my lesson - I never quit another job without having a *better* job to go to.

I found such a job not much more than a month after going to work at McDonald's, when I was hired to collect on delinquent accounts for Heilig Meyers. My boss there - Mr. Wayne Cooper - was a good Christian man, always pleasant to be around. The Credit Manager at Heilig Meyers nicknamed me "Stick" because I learned to drive a 5-speed truck to get the job. It wasn't the best job, and I wasn't fond of collecting money or repossessing furniture from folks who were often as poor as *we* were (and who were being charged exorbitant interest rates), but I consoled myself with the knowledge that God gives us all free will, and that people make bad choices, and that there are repercussions to those choices.

I've seen a *lot* of that during my law enforcement career. Sadly, to a much more tragic degree.

My next job was for S&S Loan Service. It was the same kind of job, but I was called a "chaser," and I didn't have to repossess any furniture. When Mickey Stewart at Farmers Furniture in Waynesboro offered me twenty-five cents more per hour to work there, I took it. I learned a lot from Mickey. He was friendly, very personable, and treated all his customers – black and white – equally, and with grace and good will. He set a good example. He got me a job as Credit Manager at the Farmers Furniture in Sylvania, where I worked with Jim Finch. Another great guy, Mr. Finch was cool and always fun to be around.

These jobs weren't ideal, but I believe they were all a part of the plan, and that I learned a lot about dealing with people – especially people who didn't particularly want to deal with *me*.

Most of these high school jobs were full time – I was on a work/study program at Burke Comprehensive High School from the tenth through the twelfth grades, so I got out of school at 12:30 each day and went to work.

I didn't care much for high school, although I had several teachers and counselors who took an interest in me: great educators like Mr. Roland Tuff and Ms. Jeanette Tindal, Mrs. Patricia Roberts, Mrs. Brenda Jones and Mrs. Ellen Brigham, Mrs. Linda Dunaway, Dr. Andrew Russell, Mr. Harrison Simpson and Mrs. Deborah Ide. Mrs. Roberts and Mrs. Jones saw to it that I received a $500 technical school scholarship upon graduation. I didn't use the scholarship (I wound up not furthering my education until I was thirty), but just the fact that they thought I was *worthy* of it made me feel good and really encouraged me.

Mr. Tuff, my Social Studies teacher (who in later years became a good friend), told me that he often worried about me in high school. He said I just seemed so quiet and depressed, and he feared I might harm myself. I was just always thinking about work. I didn't have time for all the socializing and nonsense which made up the after-school lives of most of my classmates.

The high school football coach, C.B. Cornett, tried to get me to play football. "Let *Alonzo* work," he told me.

I nearly laughed in his face. "Man, are you kidding? *I* got to work!"

I forget how many push-ups he made me do after that, but it almost made me throw up.

So, I worked. And saved. And told myself that as soon as I graduated, I was going to apply to the police department.

My senior year in high school (when I was eighteen), my mother, brother Alonzo, and myself bought a house. *Our* house. It's a four-bedroom, two-bath home at 310 Larry Drive. It's our *family* home, and where my mother lives to this day.

Definitely something to say Grace over.

Our Family Home

CHAPTER FIVE
Augusta PD Badge #287

It's not all that unusual for a young boy to dream of becoming a police officer. Like astronauts and cowboys and race car drivers, law enforcement is one of those jobs which holds the promise of excitement and notoriety, mixed with – perhaps more so in the case of wearing a badge – an element of authority. I just knew that the police *helped* people.

I don't recall a time where I played "cops and robbers" with my neighborhood friends that I wasn't a "cop." My sisters will tell stories of me standing in the hallway of the house on Pilgrim Way each morning before school, directing traffic as we all hurried to get ready to catch the number sixty-five bus. I spent a great deal of time talking to police officers and sheriff's deputies whenever I saw them at the station or in town or each year at the

Me and my oldest sister Angela. I'm already trying to look the part of plainclothes detective.

Exchange Club Fair. Lt. Willie Lockhart, Officer Curt St. Germaine, Sgt. Charles Gibbons, and others were great inspirations and would take the time to "talk shop" with me, sometimes even giving me rides home in their patrol vehicles – always a thrill!

So it was that - shortly after my graduation from Burke County Comprehensive High School in May of 1990 – I walked into the City of Augusta Police Department and picked up an application. (Although the Waynesboro PD was closer, I felt

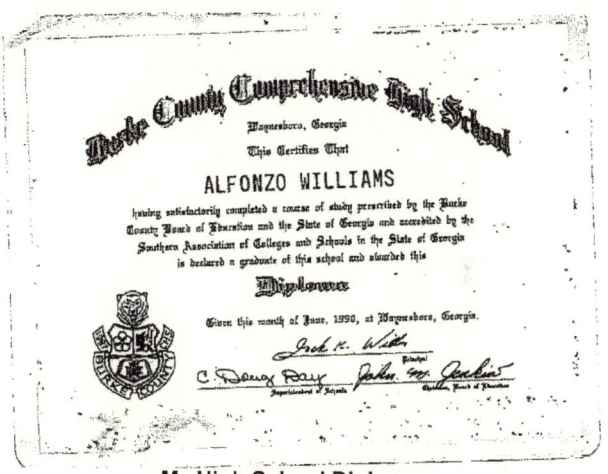

My High School Diploma

the "big city" offered more opportunities and excitement. And, honestly, I didn't want to be arresting childhood friends). Libby, who oversaw HR at the APD, took a liking to me, and I was thorough and prompt throughout the hiring process. That being said, it was a *long* way from a "smooth ride."

I'm often asked – as a young African-American male raised in the projects in the Deep South – how racism affected me, how it perhaps created barriers which wouldn't have existed if not for the color of my skin. I honestly didn't think about it too much – it wasn't really an issue at school, as the student population was representative of the demographics of the town (about half black and half white, with a sprinkling of Hispanic Americans). I *do* remember the feeling of being closely watched at the convenience store, or at the Family Dollar or the Piggly Wiggly. But Momma always told us to be respectful, to not put our hands on things we weren't going to buy – in short, not to do anything to validate prejudiced preconceptions.

I remember that Dr. Green's office had two separate entrances, and that we were always told to use one *particular* entrance when we went. Of course, I had to find out what went on behind that *other* door. My young imagination conjured up scenes of surgery or autopsies on that day I defied my mother's orders, but it was much less exciting than that: It was simply the entrance to the white folks' waiting room. The nurse, Bellsheba Dent, scolded me, and my curiosity was disappointingly sated. (She was a good nurse, though – I particularly recall a time when I thought I was going deaf and she cured me by removing some wax from my ear).

I recall that we all swam at the nearby Davis Park pool, and that we weren't welcome at the Jones Pool on the white side of town, and that it was generally accepted that – come Exchange Club Fair time – Tuesday nights were "Whites night" while we had Wednesdays and Saturdays.

I didn't think of any of this as particularly "racist." I just thought that it was how things *were*. I certainly wasn't going to waste time worrying over something I had absolutely no control over.

So it was quite a stunning blow when racism – or at least stereotyping - almost derailed my law enforcement career before it even began, and that it was perpetuated by a *black* woman.

She was the Captain of Detectives, a neat, small-framed woman perhaps jaded by Burke County's reputation at the time (mainly thanks to a well-known local family who trafficked narcotics from New York to Florida to North Carolina and Georgia) as a "Drug Capital." As she escorted me to take my pre-employment polygraph test, she looked over my application.

"Oh, you're from Burke County," she said. "Have you ever seen or taken drugs?"

I answered honestly: "No ma'am. My mother didn't play that kind of stuff. She would kill us."

"You're a damned liar," she told me.

When I protested and swore I was being honest, that I'd only seen drugs in the newspaper or on TV, she said, "Well, we'll see about that."

Looking back, I understand her skepticism: Although she was black herself, she'd been in law enforcement for a few years, and when you deal primarily with one *segment* (the criminal element) of a demographic, you can – if not ever-vigilant – develop a bias. And while I harbor no grudges (her daughter actually works with me now at the Burke County Sheriff's Department), at the time it was like a literal punch in my already nervous gut. I thought a lifetime of dreams was going up in smoke right out of the gate. I thought I'd failed the test before I'd even taken it.

In a sense, I had.

There are lots of factors which play into how well we do when hooked up to a machine and told to tell the truth, with our futures and lives on the line. Nervousness is definitely one of those factors (despite those "control" questions they ask to set the graph's parameters), and I'd never *been* so nervous: the woman who was giving me this crucial test already thought me a "damned liar."

It's a funny story to tell, and almost sounds like it could be an SNL sketch. It wasn't funny *at all* then.

When I completed the exam, sure enough, she told me I'd failed.

"No, ma'am, I'm telling you the truth," I pleaded. "There's no *way* I could have failed!"

My pleas fell on deaf, uncaring ears. After all, her mind was already made up.

"Well, I'm not going to discuss it with you," she said. "I'll turn in the results to the hiring board."

What followed were perhaps the longest days of my life, as I replayed that polygraph in my mind a thousand times, wondered how I could have maybe re-framed my honest answers in a way which would have *registered* as honesty. Wondered what I was going to do with my life if I couldn't follow my dreams. The military? Maybe back into the grocery business? I had my whole life in front of me, with the only option I truly *wanted* in the hands of strangers who probably thought as little of me as the woman who administered that test.

A week or so later I was called in front of the hiring board, this group of about ten incredibly somber and serious individuals. If anything, I was even *more* nervous this time. At least I wasn't hooked up to a machine.

"Why'd you fail the polygraph test?" was one of the first questions they asked me.

"Sir," I said, addressing the man who'd asked, "I *didn't* fail the polygraph. I failed one *question*, and she called me a liar."

"Well, you don't fail 'one question,'" he replied. "You either pass the test or you don't."

I was terrified. I pleaded once again.

"Please understand, I grew up in the projects, but I'm from the country," I said. "My mother was very strict, and she just didn't tolerate any foolishness." I told them I'd been working pretty much full-time since I was fifteen – that I just didn't hang out, socialize, go to pep rallies or sporting events, or anything that would even put me in the *proximity* of that stuff.

"I just *work*," I said.

I saw a couple of heads nodding, notes being taken, but there was really no way to get a read on them. Finally, I was dismissed.

The anxiety was shorter-lived this time.

The next day, I got a call at work from Debbie Reed, secretary for then-Augusta Chief of Police Freddie Lott.

"Can you come in to meet with the chief?" she asked.

"I'll be right there!" I said.

It was about an hour and fifteen-minute drive from my office in Sylvania to the police station. I was still as nervous as I could possibly be, but this time with a little more excitement than dread. After all, surely the chief wouldn't want to see me just to tell me I *didn't* get the job. Surely that would have been done with just a phone call (probably from Capt. "You're a Damned Liar").

One of the first questions Chief Lott – a ruddy, middle-aged redneck-looking man – asked me was, "Why'd you fail the polygraph?"

I answered as I'd answered numerous times already – every bit as honestly, if now better-rehearsed and a bit more confidently.

He listened intently, nodding throughout, gauging me it seemed.

When I finished, he asked, "Boy, where'd you go to school?"

I told him I'd graduated from Burke County High School.

"No, no," he said. "Where'd you go to *college*?"

I told him I'd never *been* to college; that I didn't really aspire to higher education. That all I'd ever wanted was to get into the police academy, and then to become a detective.

"Huh," he said. "You talk like you've been to college."

One of the traits instilled in us kids by our mother is speaking clearly and distinctly, particularly when addressing authority figures. Slang is okay around family and friends (and we can lay it on *thick* when it's just us), but it's disrespectful in anything but the most informal of settings. Some folks in the projects thought that we "put on airs" or that we considered ourselves as "better" because of this. Nonsense. It's all about respect. It shows that you're thinking about what you're saying, and that you respect your audience enough to make the effort to communicate clearly. And that's what I did on *that* day.

"Well, I like you," Chief Lott said. "I think I'm gonna give you a chance."

There are moments which we define in our memories as turning points, those instances which separate one period of our lives and the next. It was on this August day in 1990, three months out of high school and with the aid and approval of a man who would follow every step of my career and become a role model and friend, that my childhood ended.

Not long after that, I pinned on Augusta Police Department badge number 287.

Proudly wearing APD Badge #287

CHAPTER SIX
Aiming to Succeed

"Boy, you couldn't hit the broad side of a barn...you might want to think about gettin' a job at McDonald's."

These weren't exactly the most *encouraging* words to a new recruit (particularly one who'd *already* worked at a McDonald's), but it was a theme I'd hear from the Augusta Police Department firearms instructors often over the course of my first few days on the job.

In hindsight, I completely understand why Sergeants Karl Hydrick and Jackie Klaus were so tough on the new guys: We were the ones who would be backing up their brothers and sisters in blue on the streets, and mistakes could – and *did* – have catastrophic consequences. But they also just didn't understand why someone who didn't already know how to shoot would even *want* to get into law enforcement.

My first week as a police officer was a whirlwind: thrilling and exciting, but mingled with flurries of doubt and dread and disappointment. It all started (of course) with paperwork, then with a visit to the Quartermaster, Sgt. Tommy Hammock – an overweight, sarcastic, long-time veteran of the force, riding out his years to retirement handing out equipment and uniforms during the day and working security detail for high school ball games and other community events nights and weekends. Sgt. Hammock gave me my badge and stainless steel .38 revolver, then opened a closet full of used uniforms and told me to find my size.

That was the "thrilling and exciting" part. Then I went to what was affectionately known as "the range classroom."

Located in an old wooden building on a dirt-and-gravel road running parallel to I-20 on the Georgia-South Carolina border about five miles outside of Augusta, the range classroom was where we learned what we needed to know before stepping out onto the firing range. We were taught about the seven fundamentals of shooting: sight picture, sight alignment, trigger squeeze, grip, stance, breath and follow through. We also learned about "use of force" laws, which basically define what the police can do to compel compliance by an unwilling subject – this covered areas like when it was okay to shoot a fleeing suspect or felon, the laws on "stop and frisk," and how much force was allowed, and when.

We were instructed to assess every potentially lethal situation using the acronym AOJ: *Ability* (referring to the suspect's capability to injure or kill you), *Opportunity* (whether the circumstances are such that the suspect would *use* that ability), and *Jeopardy* (whether the suspect's actions or words lead to a reasonable belief that he or she *intends* to injure or kill you).

As I took it all in, the gravity of what I was learning started to sink in. I was coming to grips with the idea that part of my chosen career was the possibility that I might one day have to end a life.

It only got heavier out on the firing range.

About 90% of cadets who flunk out of the academy fail due to firearms testing, and much of what was required in that initial training was to assess whether we'd be able to handle the testing at the academy.

Until I was hired as a police officer, I'd never even *handled* a firearm. It was one of those "guy" things that – as a boy growing up with no real father-figure - I'd just not been exposed to beyond what I'd seen on TV, watching "C.H.I.P.S." or "Cagney & Lacey" or "The Dukes of Hazard." This was immensely more real.

Firing at those green and white silhouettes, concentrating on putting holes in their center mass (that part of the human body which holds most of the vital organs) or – with the *failure drill* (as in "failure to stop" – it was originally called the "Mozambique drill" from its origins following that country's war for independence) – putting two shots in the center mass followed by one to the head, helped drive the seriousness of it all home.

It was a rocky start, but I've now been a firearms *instructor* for twenty-seven years

It was stressful to a peace-loving country boy, and it didn't help that I sensed that the training officers didn't have much tolerance for my unfamiliarity with weapons. In addition to yelling at me about my marksmanship (or lack thereof) and suggesting career alternatives in fast food, their *instructions* to me conflicted: I'd hear "you're not understanding sight alignment" or "your stance is off" from one, while another right behind him would tell me my difficulties lay in my breathing or jerking (instead of squeezing) the trigger.

With a couple of the recruits – mainly those whom I felt the trainers were more eager to help pass – they utilized a variation of what's called "Kentucky windage." Usually the term refers to adjusting your aim to compensate for the wind (i.e., if you've got a strong left-to-right wind, you aim to the left of your target based upon factors such as wind speed and distance of the target), but in this case it meant that the trainer - upon seeing that a recruit was consistently missing, say, high left would get the recruit to simply *aim* low right. They weren't correcting the problem which was causing the inaccuracy, they were *adapting* the inaccuracy to reach the ultimate goal of passing the test.

In order to be certified with our firearm, we had to score an 80 on two consecutive firing range tests. Fortunately, they allowed plenty of time and practice (even though their impatience was obvious), and I was able to get my certification. It was also during this time that I learned how to handle my baton, the basics of pepper spraying, and night shooting.

Not bad for my first week, I thought.

CHAPTER SEVEN
Fatherhood and Finances

In the summer of 1990, it seemed like the new decade was off to a great start: Not only had I landed my dream job with the Augusta Police Department, but I was about to become a father!

Tarsha (my first daughter's mother) was a high school sweetheart. I'd met her at Piggly Wiggly bagging groceries for her family, who were regular customers. Mine and Tarsha's relationship had never been what you'd call *healthy* – she had jealousy issues, and I was intensely focused on work and career. We argued a lot, but we were just kids (then kids *with* a kid). I'm not sure I knew *how* to be a partner in a healthy relationship. I hadn't really seen that much growing up. It didn't help that her family didn't really like me – they were among those I mentioned previously who seemed to think that my family thought that we were "better" than other poor families. That was my own perception, and I know I could be wrong.

Despite all this, there is no joy quite like the joy of becoming a parent for the first time. I was a proud and happy daddy when Kiara Shanese Williams was born on November 1, 1990. Sadly, her birth didn't do much to reconcile the differences between her mother and me. We hadn't married (I'm not proud of that, but I wouldn't have been proud about being divorced either), and our relationship was irreparably damaged by the time Kiara was born. Tarsha refused to go back to

NOT HERE TO BE SERVED

school and I couldn't quite understand that unwillingness to better herself – something which was ingrained in me. And I'm sure she couldn't quite understand my focus on career, to the detriment of my family life. So we ended it. I vowed to be a good father- to do right by my little girl - and I believe I did, although there were some rough economic times ahead.

Even the most seemingly upright and level-headed nineteen-year-old is *still* a nineteen-year-old, and I made mistakes and had lapses of judgment in many areas of my life for which I make no excuses - only apologies. These aren't mistakes I'd make today and are all mistakes from which I learned valuable lessons.

With Kiara

Of course, my *daughter* wasn't a mistake – she was, and still *is*, one of the great blessings of my life. But I probably could have handled things better with her mother, as I could have better handled the economic hardship which was coming my way.

I bought a new car, a 1989 4-door Mitsubishi Mirage. It wasn't fancy or extravagant, but it was sleek and good on gas. My starting salary at the APD was $17,288, and I was bursting with the enthusiasm and invincibility of a young man on the rise, so I didn't really crunch the numbers.

Ironically - although I'd been working since an early age and had saved enough money to buy my first car and then go in with Momma and Alonzo on a house – I wasn't really good with finances. Momma had always taken care of the bills – we just gave her our small share.

I had been at my new job less than six months when my car was repossessed from the parking lot of the APD. ("Hey Alfonzo, it looks like they're towing your car," I was told by a fellow officer). I had to buy a used car at a much higher interest rate. Shortly thereafter, a lawyer Terrance Leiden - talked me into filing Chapter 13 bankruptcy, which was later updated to Chapter 7, eliminating payroll deductions to my secured debtors. I just signed the papers, not discovering until years later that I really *had* little debt (less than $9000), and that I could have avoided the stigma of a bankruptcy altogether. Another hard-earned lesson.

As disheartening as those incidents were, my financial woes had just begun, and would continue to be a cloud hanging over my head for the next decade.

I'd been paying child support regularly for some time when I was notified that I'd have to repay the government assistance Tarsha had – unbeknownst to me – been receiving the whole time. I got into trouble with the IRS when it was discovered that both Tarsha and I had claimed Kiara on our taxes.

I wasn't going to let my Celica Supra get repossessed!

As I was paying child support, I'd asked (and received) permission from her to file that way. During the audit, I was treated extremely rudely and condescendingly by the young black woman assigned my case. I let my anger and frustration get the better of me, and I stormed out of the office, telling her to just send me a bill.

Big mistake. The bill they sent me was for $5000, more than a quarter of my yearly salary.

I didn't have a bank account and was reduced to cashing my check at one of those check-cashing places which prey on people in my type of situation and charge exorbitant fees. I was renting my furniture at loan-shark rates from a rental store. I'd become exactly the type of person I'd spent years (both with the loan company and the furniture stores) collecting money from.

I'd fallen into the poverty trap.

My "dream job" was, at least in the first year or so, somewhat less than dreamy itself. In those days at the Augusta Police Department, new recruits were allowed to be on "field patrol" for up to a year before being required to go to the Police Academy, which held classes three times yearly. I was slated for the academy the following January and assigned Stan Ashmore as my Field Training Officer, or "FTO," in the interim.

On the day I started work, Stan went on a several weeks-long honeymoon. After my initial training, I was allowed to ride occasionally with other officers, but mostly sat - with my shiny new gun and badge - at the operator's desk, taking non-emergency phone calls. Eventually, Stan returned from his honeymoon and I got to ride with him every day.

People will often ask about the first time I responded to the scene of a violent crime or my first arrest or the first time I drew my gun in the line of duty. I wish I could remember, but I can't. The crack epidemic sweeping the country was in full-force in the early '90s, and Augusta was – like many cities – ravaged by violence. It wasn't uncommon to draw your weapon a couple of times a week or more, and I made arrests on a regular basis from the outset. As far as recalling my first violent crime scene, I think that many of us in law enforcement develop a certain detachment from the blood and the violence. I also believe that – for me at least – I was just too young to have a true understanding of the value of human life, of the momentous impact of such tragedy. The older I get, the less detached I become, and the more I understand the preciousness and fleetingness of life. It's difficult now for me *not* to get emotional when I see some of the horrors which are a part of my chosen career.

> **MIRANDA WARNING**
> 1. You have the right to remain silent.
> 2. Anything you say can and will be used against you in a court of law.
> 3. You have the right to talk to a lawyer and have him present with you while you are being questioned.
> 4. If you cannot afford to hire a lawyer, one will be appointed to represent you before any questioning, if you wish.
> 5. You can decide at any time to exercise these rights and not answer any questions or make any statements.

The famous "Miranda Warning." We were highly encouraged to read this whether we had it memorized or not.

Although I can't quite recall some of the "firsts" of my career, there are a couple I'll never forget:

I was riding with Stan Ashmore when I was made my first successful radio call. It was "10-76 RCJ One 10-95," which meant that we were in route to the Richmond County Jail with one prisoner. It was a big moment for me – I'd been studying those codes, both at home and during many hours of riding with Stan (most FTOs preferred doing the driving), and being able to put my learning to use was a thrill.

In December of 1990, after less than five months on the job, I went to my first funeral for a fallen officer.

Tommy Hammock, the sergeant in the Quartermaster's office who'd given me my uniform, badge, and gun, was robbed and shot to death outside of his apartment complex, "Damascus Woods." As of just that previous October, it was also where *I* lived. Sgt. Hammock had just finished working a security detail at a high school basketball game when he was killed. It was such a tragedy and underscored what a dangerous city I lived and worked in.

The funeral service, which filled the 1200-seat church to capacity, underscored the bond of the law enforcement community.

Damascus Woods offered reduced rent to some police officers in exchange for helping with issues such as handing out late notices, giving excessive noise warnings, etc. I wound up taking over Sgt. Hammock's duties there. Life can just be surreal.

Despite all the drama – both on and off the job – I had hope, and I had faith I was where God wanted me to be.

In January of 1991, He wanted me at the Augusta Police Academy.

CHAPTER EIGHT

The Academy

My plan had been to ace the police academy – housed in those days in the Martha Lester School in Augusta, under the auspices of the Richmond County Public School System – when I started classes in January of 1991. I felt that I had some stereotypes to overcome, both as a kid from the projects (which I'd already faced with the polygraph fiasco) and as a country bumpkin from a county ten times smaller than Augusta, where we waved at neighbors and strangers and police alike. (If you waved at an APD officer back then, you'd more than likely just attract suspicion).

I thought the greatest hurdles to my law enforcement career were behind me.

Boy was I wrong.

I have to be honest – my less-than-stellar performance as a cadet was partly my own doing. I was distracted by a girl. It's a bit ironic, actually, that – after splitting with Tarsha in part because of my unwavering focus on my career (and swearing that I was done with relationships) – it was a lack of focus due to a relationship which threatened (again) to *derail* my career.

I'd met Stephanie at Hardee's, where Officer Robert Owens (my FTO for that day) and I were getting biscuits and coffee on a cold morning. She'd jaywalked crossing the road (she worked at that Hardee's), and I joked with her about violating the law. We hit it off.

It was this particular distraction which led to me coming in late from lunch, sleeping in class, and just not paying as much attention as I should have been. But I had some other hurdles as well: I quickly learned that – despite my love of law enforcement, my countless chats with police officers and sheriff's deputies growing up, and the dozens of arrests I'd made in my first five months on the job – I knew amazingly *little* about the criminal justice system. I'm not proud to admit this, but I didn't even know exactly what a *district attorney* was, or what they did!

In a six-week period, we had to learn criminal law, juvenile law, constitutional law, traffic law, investigations, interrogations, mental health, use of force, search and seizure, and other topics – all really crammed down our throats. We had a test every Monday on the material we'd learned the previous week. This was all in addition to the forty hours of firearms training (not nearly as stressful as the first time around, but still with the confusion of getting different advice from different instructors), forty hours of self-defense, and eight hours of CPR. These days the course is *eleven* weeks long. For good reason.

I felt like I was in college (one with a *really* tough Phys Ed curriculum, which included training with a martial arts expert – a small Asian man who knew how to *hurt* you), and that I was in *way* over my head. I had to fight the urge daily to give in or give up, telling myself again and again that this was my *dream*, the career path I'd been preparing for my whole life, and that it had to – at some point – get easier. And that even if it didn't, my only choices were to adapt or quit. And quitting just wasn't an option.

I also comforted myself with the knowledge that the powers-that-be really *wanted* us to succeed. During the crack/crime epidemic of the early '90s, the law enforcement environment was similar to what it is now: We were at odds with much of the community, judged as a whole by the bad actions of a few. We always had targets on our backs, and it was getting tougher and tougher to find people who even *wanted* to be officers at a time when *more* were desperately needed.

There were about thirty of us in the class of January-March of '91, taught by a Captain, a Lieutenant, and several adjunct instructors, all overseen by a Colonel. I don't recall that any of the class flunked out. There were awards given at graduation for things like "Top Academic" (this went to an older guy who'd been with the State Park Police) and "Top Gun" (as the name implies, this went to the guy – ex-military - who'd received the highest scores on the firing range).

Much like in my high school days - which seemed like much longer than a mere ten months prior - I came out average. But where in high school I'd at least received a *few* awards ("Most Dependable," "Most Courteous," and "Friendliest"), there were no such honors to distinguish me much from my fellow cadets.

On that day in March of 1991, I didn't need to be distinguished from the other cadets – it was enough that I was distinguished from the boy who'd grown up with the dream of graduating from the Police Academy.

Because I *had*.

NOT HERE TO BE SERVED

March 1991 Graduating Class of the Police Academy at Martha Lester School. I'm in the 3rd row, 2nd from left.

CHAPTER NINE

Field Training Officer Williams

Very early in my law enforcement career, I learned that the majority of police officers fall into one of two camps: crime fighters and social workers. The former group gets into police work because they want to catch bad guys. They want action. These are the aggressive ones and – honestly – the type most prone to give our profession a bad name. Those in the latter group get into it because they feel a sense of civic responsibility – they want to help people, to be *of service*.

I've always considered it a badge of honor to count myself as the "social worker" type. I've always wanted to be more of a role model and inspiration than a tough guy, and believe that in doing this I can truly make a *difference* in society, even if I'm only affecting a single person at a time.

Of course, the reality is that – even in a high-crime area like Augusta, Georgia in the early '90s – most police work is social work. We spend a great deal more time *serving* than *protecting*. That doesn't sound nearly as glamorous or exciting as being a "crime fighter," but any officer who tells you any different is either pulling your leg or their *own*.

Yes, our lives are on the line every day. It's our duty to go into situations normal people would run from. And, sadly, we often have targets on our backs just because of the job we do. But that's really only a very small part of the equation.

Those in law enforcement who provided me the greatest inspiration, who served as role models for my own career, were the social worker-types. Stan Ashmore was one of these, and I learned a lot from him, both before the Academy and during the eight weeks afterward, when he was once again my FTO (this would be my last stint as a "trainee").

It was at about this time that the APD added a driving course, one which hadn't been part of the curriculum at the academy, but which would now be required. It was called the "Emergency Vehicles Operations Course," and if you couldn't pass it, you had to walk a beat (known as a "901").

In my thirty years in law enforcement, *this* was the most difficult challenge.

I wasn't a *bad* driver by any means – driving had been a big part of several of my jobs before I joined the force – but this course was *something else*! They held the EVOC training sessions every three days at the Georgia Public Safety Training Center, an intense series of maneuvers around and between (and often *over*) those orange cones, simulating wet conditions and kids running out in the road and all sorts of hazards and obstacles, culminating in a timed test.

I failed it three times.

There's a chance I *may* have passed sooner if not for my mouth. The instructor for that session was a big, buff ladies' man who seemed more intent on hitting on the young female officers than teaching the course. I probably shouldn't have confronted him about it (you'd think I'd have learned that after the Piggly Wiggly incident).

The timed test required you to complete a series of maneuvers in two minutes and thirty seconds. If you completed it in two minutes and thirty-*one* seconds, you failed. And, of course, the instructor was holding the stopwatch. I should've kept my mouth shut.

But I was determined and resolute, and had an ally in the training department who kept sending me back and pushing me forward, encouraging me the whole way. On the fourth try, I passed.

I don't necessarily *enjoy* facing obstacles, but I love *overcoming* them. As with my firearms training - in which I became an instructor in 1993, and have since helped hundreds of officers get certified - so too did I conquer this challenge, and became a defensive driving instructor in 2005.

My mouth also threatened to get me in trouble in another area of police work - testifying in court. As the arresting officer on a case, you often become the target of desperate defense attorneys' attempts to paint you and your work in a negative light in their efforts to find some sort of procedural error which might set their client free. It's therefore understandable that a somewhat adversarial relationship often exists between those attorneys and the law enforcement community.

Judge Carl Brown

I wasn't having any of that. In my youthful pride, I saw the defense attorneys' attempts at legal wrangling as an assault on my integrity and professionalism. As a threat to my career. It took Judge Carl Brown to make me realize that my *attitude* was the greater threat.

"You've got to stop arguing with those attorneys," he told me in his chambers. He instilled in me a deeper understanding of the criminal justice system, and that it was every bit as much the job of the attorneys to defend their clients as it was my job to arrest them.

I took Judge Brown's advice to heart, and a couple of years later he wrote Chief Lott a glowing letter about what a highly professional witness I had become. That Judge and I are friends to this day – he's the Superior Court Judge for the district which includes Burke County. We campaigned together in 2016. We both won. And, over the years, I've become an expert at testifying. I've taught it. I've had defense attorneys try to use it against me to try to counteract the effectiveness of looking juries in the eye and speaking clearly and calmly.

Difficulties with recruiting – due in part to an intense 600-question psychological exam and rigorous screening, both of which have been rolled back since - and a high rate of attrition at the time combined to make it so that, if you had a couple of years on the force, you were almost a senior officer (even if it wasn't necessarily reflected in your rank). This, along with a driving ambition and strict adherence to protocol, led to me becoming an FTO within a year of leaving the Academy.

It was very gratifying working with new recruits who were as excited as I had been (and still was) at becoming a police officer. It also provided quite a few adventures.

I was training a new Academy graduate – a small-framed woman with a ponytail tied in a bun and an almost-grandmotherly disposition, a kind and caring spirit who certainly embodied the social worker-type officer – when we spotted a stolen vehicle on 15th Street. We got behind the car to conduct a felony stop. They fled.

After a high-speed chase (I thanked God for the driving course), I managed to get the suspects blocked off in a cul-de-sac. I leapt from the patrol car, gun drawn, ordering the driver and passengers to show me their hands. It was an incredibly tense moment – not just for me and (I assume) the suspects, but also for my trainee. Maybe even more so – once the situation was contained, I found her crouched down in the floorboard of the cruiser.

As I mentioned in an article in the *Augusta Chronicle* that year, sometimes all you can do is pray. I went out and bought a gospel tape that day.

Another incident during my time as an FTO, and one which was probably among the scariest of my early days on the force, was a stakeout at a single-story shotgun house on Conklin Street, in the 12th and Old Savannah Road area (like 15th Street in the previous tale, this was part of what was known as

A 1992 *Augusta Chronicle* article about prayer in the line of duty.

the "#2 Beat" – the section of Augusta with the highest crime rate). We'd answered a domestic disturbance call at the address, and found a woman severely beaten. Before we got the victim off to the ER, she'd told us that she expected her boyfriend – the perp – to return.

The Officer-in-Charge at the scene, Sgt. Lee Woods, suggested I stay in the house and wait, with my trainee staged out of sight nearby.

It was one of the longest nights of my career. The house was filthy, cold, and dark, and the minutes seemed like days as I awaited the return of a dangerous felon. It was like being in a horror movie, but without the ominous music.

As is the case with most police work, the end was rather anti-climactic: The suspect never showed. Like the old Tom Petty song, the waiting was the hardest part.

Ironically, the part of Augusta with second highest crime rate is called the "#1 Beat." Officer Grace Wittke - a tall, solidly-built woman who hadn't joined the force until she was in her forties - was training with me the night we received a dispatch to the 700 block of Demaret Street in the Delta Manor Housing Project. A woman reported that her brother was high on some type of drugs - possibly PCP - and he was hallucinating. She said he had busted the glass window of the back door and cut himself very badly.

We arrived at the scene within a few minutes of the call, and found her brother – a 5'7" 165-pound black male – wandering around in the yard, bleeding profusely from gashes which had peeled back the skin on his arm. We called in a 10-52, 10-18 (need an ambulance, need it *now*), and attempted to further assess the man's condition. He became combative and we attempted to subdue him until the ambulance arrived, using every means at our disposal – including our batons. Although each of us was bigger, he had the strength we often see exhibited by those under the influence of drugs (particularly those like PCP), and we had to call for back-up. It took all of us, with the help of the EMTs who'd arrived at the scene, to get the man handcuffed to the stretcher.

As is protocol in such a situation, several of us officers followed the ambulance to University Hospital, where we helped get the patient from the stretcher to a bed in a section of the ER designed for such prisoner-patients. Getting him strapped to the bed presented its own challenge, and the attending physician didn't care for our methods. He asked us to step back and allow him to try and calm the patient. None of us officers present said "I told you so" when the man broke the straps and unloaded a glob of phlegm into the doctor's face, but we *could* have.

We once again helped restrain the patient, the medical team was able to get him sedated, and we were able to leave. We *thought* it was over.

Grace and I were still doing paperwork when we got the call to return to the ER. The attending physician had issued a Form 1013, which allowed the man to be detained and sent for mental health treatment at Georgia Regional Hospital. The patient's injuries had been treated and he was still sedated when we got him *into* the car, but the sedation apparently wore off in route. There were six members of the hospital staff awaiting us at GRH. They too asked us to let them handle it, concerned that perhaps the man's aggressive behavior was directed at us. Once again, we sighed inwardly and complied. That didn't work out so well: It took *all* of us to get him from the cruiser to his padded room.

We didn't say "I told you so" then, either. But we could have.

I was riding solo (working the #2 Beat) the night of the firefight at the Blue Note club, a notorious blue-block building on Old Savannah Road. I recall seeing what seemed like a couple hundred people running out of the building, seeing muzzle flashes from inside amidst a cacophony of gunfire, hearing the shattering of bullet-riddled windshields and headlights from my perch behind the wheel well of my cruiser.

Several people were taken to the ER that night, but there were no fatalities. As this was a time when Augusta's violent crime rate was as high as it had been in the city's history, I'm not sure this one even made the papers.

It wasn't just the crime rate which made the environment for police so hostile in the early '90s: We were perceived as "the Enemy" by a large part of the community – particularly the African-American community. I've always found it disheartening that, as a black law enforcement officer, I'm often perceived as an "Uncle Tom" or even called a traitor to my race. There's nothing I can do about such misperceptions except to try every day to dispel them, even if only one person at a time. I've learned from sad experience that hatred of law enforcement has nothing to do with black and white – only blue.

I had no idea how much worse it was about to get.

On Wednesday, April 29th, 1992 I was working as an FTO with Officer Jorge Garcia (now Jo Martin), who had recently joined the APD after relocating to Augusta from New Jersey. We got a call from dispatch to go to the Allen Holmes Apartments regarding a fight where an adult male was alleged to have hit a juvenile. Upon arrival, we spoke with the victim's mother, who pointed toward a small group of black males gathered beneath a large oak tree outside the apartment complex.

Confrontations like this were an everyday part of the job. Neither Officer Garcia nor I anticipated anything beyond routine.

Then again, neither of us had heard about the verdict in the Rodney

King case.

It's rare to get such breaking news from a potential suspect, but in this case the word seemed to spread more quickly through the black community than through law enforcement.

"Man, we're already pissed off about the Rodney King verdict," one of the men said when asked about the assault on the minor. "Don't come over here with that bullshit!"

We told them, truthfully, that we hadn't heard a thing about the verdict and that, besides, this had *nothing whatsoever* to do with it. After a brief argument, one of the men challenged Garcia to take off his gun belt and fight. "I'll kick your ass," he told my partner.

Garcia had worked for the police department in New Jersey and was certified to carry a "handler," which was a defensive tactical piece – a side-handled baton - common up North, but mostly unfamiliar to law enforcement in the South. When he took this off, I thought I was about to see how it was used. But then he took off his gun belt as well.

There was going to be a fight.

I begged Garcia not to do it, but he was as stubborn as I was. And once *he* started fighting, it was my duty to join in. As we waited on back-up to arrive, the fighting intensified, and the crowd grew. Officer Darryl Hamilton arrived and joined in, then Officer Byron Thomas. Then others.

We could hear the sirens of *more* back-up converging on a scene which threatened to become a full-on riot. We didn't know that such riots were at that very moment breaking out all over the *country*.

That's when Officer Hamilton fetched his Remington 270 shotgun and fired it into the air. While a violation of departmental regulations, and one which could well have turned a street brawl into a firefight, it did the trick: The crowd dispersed, and we were able to make a few arrests. Apart from a broken finger suffered by Thomas and a few other minor injuries (both to officers and civilians), no one was hurt. It could have been a disaster.

Lt. Larry Vinson, the shift commander that day, wanted to fire Hamilton for his warning shot. Fortunately, I was an officer whom Vinson really liked. When I told him that Hamilton's actions had most likely saved lives, he backed down and just suspended him for a few days without pay.

As Los Angeles burned, as riots and looting continued throughout the country, I knew the coming weeks and months were going to be a real challenge for law enforcement – particularly for the men and women in blue.

I had no idea I was about to trade in *my* blue uniform for a detective's badge.

CHAPTER TEN

Making Detective

When you're an eight-year old boy living in the projects with dreams of becoming a police officer, you don't think of the details – you think of the dream. You don't think about exactly *how* the dream will come about, you don't set short- and long-term goals, you don't think about any "plan of action."

At some point during my childhood, the dreams of being a police officer and a police *detective* kind of melded together. As I grew older and started learning about goal-setting and – through TV and my chats with the various law enforcement-types whose brains I picked whenever the opportunity arose – the nuts-and-bolts of the profession, I knew that graduating the police academy was going to be the first step. I set that as my first goal. But my *ultimate* goal was to be a detective.

With all the hurdles I had to overcome throughout my first year as a member of the Augusta Police Department, there were moments when the long-term goal took a back seat to my doubts about whether I'd even be able to succeed as a patrol officer, much less move up the ladder. It took a while for me to get settled in, for my ambition to resume its rightful place on my list of priorities.

I'd been out of training and on my own for about six months when I applied for detective. I had no illusions that anything would come of it

– after all, I was only twenty years old, and I was pretty sure the APD had never even *had* a detective my age. But it never hurts to try, and each failure is just a necessary steppingstone to success.

A few months after applying, I had a conversation which would change my life.

Tony Walden and Richard Elim were the "Dynamic Duo" of the APD Detective Division. They worked violent crimes, and could have come right out of Central Casting: Elim was a huge black man, and the "Enforcer" of the pair – he was the guy who could get confessions; Walden, a slim white guy, was more the procedural and "paperwork guy." They made a great team, and had solved several high-profile cases - including the Tommy Hammock murder I mentioned.

I'd returned to the station to file some paperwork when the two detectives, standing outside the building by a trash can, called me over.

"We've been thinking about promoting some detectives," said one. "What do you think about that?"

"That's neat!" I said. There was an excited feeling in the pit of my stomach, but I wasn't going to get *too* carried away. I was sure there was another – less dream-like – explanation for this conversation.

I was wrong.

"How'd you like to come work in investigations?"

I was floored. In as good a way as being floored can get.

"Man, I've always wanted to do that. I just didn't think it would happen this fast," I told them. "Why me?"

As it turned out, they thought I'd make a good detective not because they saw in me the potential to be the Augusta version of "Shaft," but because I was damned good at paperwork.

In all the excitement about shoot-outs and car chases and catching bad guys, the role of written reports and filling out forms in police work is usually overlooked. It shouldn't be: It's probably one of the most critical aspects of law enforcement. There are a *lot* of criminals walking the streets due to sub-par paperwork. As a patrol officer, I was meticulous. I was very thorough and wrote about my interviews with victims and witnesses in such detail that the detectives who were then assigned the cases had to do very little follow-up.

Basically, I caught the attention of the detectives mainly because I'd made their work so much easier.

Yet again, my big mouth threatened to derail my progress.

"Keep this under your hat," one of the detectives told me after I'd assured them I was eager to take them up on their proposition. "Don't say anything."

It's hard to contain some levels of excitement. Officer Jerry Wutche and I worked the #1 and #2 beats together – we'd made a lot of arrests and taken a lot of drug dealers off the street. I *had* to tell Jerry.

It got back to Elim and Walden.

"We *told* you not to say anything," I was admonished. "You can't be an investigator if you can't keep your mouth shut."

I swore it would never happen again - one of the first times I dodged a bullet which my mouth shot off.

Within a few months, I was promoted. I was twenty-one.

They say that when it rains, it pours sometimes the cliché has a *positive* connotation.

Not long after my initial chat with Elim and Walden, I was approached by Detectives Roderick Berry and Horace Spratlin about joining them in Narcotics, based not as much on my writing acumen as the multiple drug arrests Wutche and I had made

My first Detective ID

(they approached Jerry about the job as well). I was somewhat torn, and went to Judge Carl Brown – who'd by now become a friend and mentor – to get his opinion. He steered me away from Narcotics, telling me that they had a rather unsavory reputation and that very few remained there for more than a few years.

It wasn't a hard sell. I went with violent crimes. Jerry went to narcotics. It was the right move for both of us. Captain Diane Wasson was still the commander of the detective division. By this time, I think I had convinced her I wasn't a liar and that I'd make a great detective. I must have, as it was her call. Although we'd had our difficulties at the outset (she was quite intimidating), I came to have the utmost respect for Captain Wasson: she was very smart, maintained a good rapport with informants, was calm under pressure, and knew her job well. She later left the agency to become chief of police for the Richmond County Board of Education, a job I would assume some twenty-two years later.

By the time I joined the detective division, Stephanie and I were no longer together. That was God's plan, for - the same month I was promoted - the woman who would become my wife (and still is today) was hired as a secretary in that division. Shirleta had just graduated with a four-year business degree from Paine College, and she'd type up my reports on rapes, robberies, murders, and child abuse cases after I had dictated them into a tape recorder. She was really good at it. Throughout our twenty-eight years together (twenty-four of them as Man and Wife), she's been my anchor, always encouraging me and pushing me to achieve my career goals, helping me navigate turbulent financial waters with common sense and pragmatism. She was the reason my previous relationships failed, for they were my steppingstones to her.

I'm also blessed to have the most wonderful in-laws – Willie and Alice Flint - one could ever hope for. They're both amazingly kind, loving, Holy Spirit-filled people. Her father - a Baptist Minister - was the first man to ever tell me he loved me. While that may seem sappy to some, it meant something to me, and the Flints helped me get over my reticence in telling friends and family – male and female – that I love them. Life is short, and not one of us is guaranteed tomorrow. If you love someone, let them know.

Shirleta Williams

I'm not the easiest man to live with: I'm not as "sharing" as I could be about some parts of my job. Part of me wants to shield Shirleta, part of me just wants to compartmentalize personal and professional. After so long together, she knows when to prod and when to back off.

I'm an incredibly blessed man.

Training as a new detective is more about learning by doing than from a structured, regimented classroom setting, although some of the classroom training was intense. Duane Christenson was the APD Crime Scene Investigator/Photographer, a huge, gruff, cigar-chomping ex-military man for whom we'd learned early on to have a cup of coffee ready when he appeared at a crime scene. He taught us new detectives about taking and developing photos ("just think of the camera as a black box"), as well as about "blood spatter analysis." We learned to tell what position the victim had been in when they were struck and how many times they'd been struck just from the patterns of their blood spatter.

Most of what I learned in training, though, I was taught by Detective Walden. I'd go out with him on follow-up investigations, where a policeman had already met with the complainant (unless it was a murder investigation, the complainant was usually the victim) and filed a report. We'd then get a "formal statement" and start filling in holes, putting pieces together, and re-interviewing witnesses - the extent to which we had to do these things was often dictated by the thoroughness of the policeman's original report. The importance of paperwork.

I learned that a criminal investigation – despite the constant advances in technology we were experiencing even then – is about 85% common sense. More than anything, it's a process of elimination: start with the love interest, then the family, then the friends. In the vast majority of cases, you don't have to go much beyond that. The bigger challenge is establishing and documenting the evidence required to get a *conviction*.

From Detective Elim, I learned about interrogation. As I mentioned, he was a really large (probably about 6'4", four hundred or so pounds) black man, raised on the #2 Beat. While not well-versed in the methods I would learn a couple of years later while in training to be an Interrogation/Interview Instructor, Elim knew the streets, and he knew *people*. He taught me about "the bottom line" – to be direct and to-the-point in interrogations, to get there quickly, and to let the suspect's body language be your guide.

Me on an APD commemorative baseball card

Elim taught me not only how to get confessions, but how to make them *stick*. Because he had a high rate of confessions - and because of his sheer *physical* presence - those confessions were almost always challenged in court (in what's called a "Jackson-Denno Hearing," which is held to determine whether the confession was voluntary, and whether it can be used as evidence).

Defense attorneys would ask questions such as "How close were you to the defendant?" and "Were you wearing your gun during the interview?" and "Did you lay your hands on the suspect?" in attempts to disqualify the confession. They rarely succeeded. Elim taught me that if you interrogate a suspect the right way, you don't *need* to rough them up.

Once I completed my training in Violent Crimes, the protocol at the time was to be transferred to the Property Crimes unit, where you'd work until you were up to snuff to be *re*-assigned to Violent Crimes. The Captain of Detectives told me to stay put. I felt this caused a bit of resentment – particularly from those detectives working property crimes but I'd already started learning to pay little attention to the social/political nuances of law enforcement.

John Padgett, who had been one of my FTOs, had been transferred to the Detective Division before me, and had been assigned to the Delinquent Juveniles/Child Abuse unit. When he was promoted to Patrol Sergeant, I took over his case load.

It was eye-opening and extremely disheartening to discover just how *many* kids were abused, and how often those abused children wound up becoming delinquents. A vicious cycle, as they themselves too frequently grow up to abuse their *own* kids. I literally worked hundreds upon hundreds – maybe as many as a thousand – of these cases.

In 1993, the Georgia State Law Enforcement Division formed the *Child Fatalities Team*, and I was asked to chair its Richmond County panel. Our role was to coordinate the efforts of various agencies in an attempt to prevent *future* deaths as much as to scrutinize *previous* cases. In the first year of the team's existence, there were – state-wide – one hundred and eighty-four such child deaths.

Of course, for every death of a child there were many, many more cases of physical and sexual abuse, so a large part of my job as a detective was investigating *these*, of helping the most innocent of victims and bringing to justice those perpetrators who – in my mind – represented the very bottom of the barrel of humanity. Whatever innocence I may have retained from my youth quickly evaporated. There had been multiple cases of sexual abuse alleged by students against teachers, and I discovered – to my dismay – a tendency of some in the teaching profession to protect their own, to make as a default assumption the dishonesty of the child and the innocence of the accused. While I'd never make a blanket generalization – as I've mentioned, several of my own teachers were tremendous inspirations – I saw it happen *way* too often.

As a large percentage of missing persons in Augusta were abused kids running away from home, the Juvenile Delinquent/Abused Child unit caught the missing persons cases as well - no matter *how* old the missing person was.

This, tragically, was how I caught my first big break.

CHAPTER ELEVEN

The Mary Colley Stewart Case

I can honestly say that I would gladly give up any accolades or awards or career advancement I've achieved as a result of a murder investigation if the clock could be wound back and the murder prevented. But that's not how the world works. It's not how *life* works. It's certainly not how death works. There are bad people out there, and their bad deeds can never be undone. All I can do is help get justice afterwards.

Robert Eugene Fielding was a bad person. He'd been a bad person his entire adult life.

Convicted for killing a gas station attendant in Augusta in May of 1969 (Fielding was just seventeen at the time of the murder), he'd been given the death penalty. He was able to get a new trial the following year, confessed this time, and was sentenced to life. He served twenty years (due to disciplinary issues, more than double the norm) and – thanks to prison overcrowding – was paroled in 1989.

Twenty-five years almost to the day after his first killing, he crossed paths with thirty-seven-year-old Mary Colley Stewart, and killed again.

On Thursday, May 12, 1994, Stewart left a note for her husband Warren (known as "Weir"), saying she'd be working late. That wasn't unusual as a Medicaid supervisor for the Richmond County Department of Family and Children's Services, she usually worked late at least one night per week. Weir and his father had attended a Green Jackets baseball game that evening and - upon returning home - Mr. Stewart was concerned to find his wife still gone. After calling some of her friends and checking with the hospital, he drove to her office. There he found her car in the parking lot. The DFACS office building was locked and seemed deserted.

His concern mounting, he went to the police station at shortly after midnight to file a Missing Person's report. He was told to return to DFACS, and that an officer would meet him there. Officer Joe Walters responded, conducted a search of the missing woman's vehicle and – with the help of the DFACS Director Pat Fitzgerald (who'd been summoned to unlock the building) – searched the offices as well. At about 3 a.m., Officer Walters handed the case over to Detective Lee Woods (the same guy who'd assigned me the stakeout of that cold dark felon's house a couple of years previously) and Sgt. Tony Walden (who'd trained me as a detective).

Noting that Mr. Stewart was slightly intoxicated (he admitted to drinking beer at the ballgame) and seeing no obvious signs of foul play, the detectives assumed – as is the case the overwhelming majority of time – that there was an innocuous explanation. Perhaps she'd gone out with friends. Perhaps she was seeing someone. Foul play was – statistically speaking – pretty far down the list of possibilities, even though Mr. Stewart was adamant that this just wasn't *like* his wife, and that she'd never done anything like this before.

At one point, while waiting for the tow truck to take Mary's car to the station for processing, Walden noticed how full the green dumpster behind the building near the loading ramp was, and made a comment to Woods about it. They didn't think anything of it at the time, and gave

Mr. Stewart a ride home. After a quick search of the house, they left.

By the time I got to work on the morning of the 13th, Mary still hadn't returned home. As someone who worked closely with DFACS in my role with the Delinquent Juvenile/Child Abuse unit, I started getting concerned calls from Mary's co-workers, imploring me to look into the case.

"Something's just not *right*," I was told.

It was still nagging at Walden and Woods as well. Sgt. Walden called Lt. Jesse Tarver, who was in charge of case assignments, and told him the case needed to be assigned to Missing Persons.

By 8:30 a.m., Lt. Tarver had given the case to me.

The DFACS office looks like a typical government office building: A faded red-brick structure which sits on a long circular drive, fronted by a well-manicured lawn and several large trees, it looks a lot like a school building.

When I arrived there that morning, it was with a guarded optimism that nothing would come of it – I expected at any moment to get the call that Mary had arrived safely home with an apology and an explanation.

The more I spoke with her co-workers, the more that optimism faded. When I discovered that the lead janitor on the night cleaning crew, Robert Fielding, was a paroled killer, I got a sick feeling in the pit of my stomach.

After conducting interviews with the DFACS staff, I discovered that Mary had last been seen by a co-worker shortly before 6 p.m. the previous evening. I discovered through interviews with other members of the cleaning crew that Fielding "hadn't been himself" that night, often disappearing for periods of time. Later interviews revealed that he'd made an effort to determine the locations of the security cameras in the building (he'd actually asked someone if a fire alarm was a camera), and that – while he was usually done working about 9 p.m. each night (as lead custodian, Fielding was the one who set the alarm), on the previous night the alarm hadn't been set until 10:39. Security records showed the rest of the cleaning crew had left at 9:15.

Over a late dinner that night, Detective Jim Gordon and I developed a theory that Fielding had killed Stewart somewhere on the premises and deposited her body in the green dumpster – the contents of which had earlier that day been taken to the landfill.

Although it was about 11 p.m., I immediately got on the phone to Linda Beasley, the Richmond County Administrator, to get permission to close the landfill. She agreed. We then tracked down the phone number for Johnny Boatright, the garbage truck driver who'd hauled away the contents of the DFACS dumpster. He agreed to meet us the next morning at the landfill to help narrow down our search parameters.

The newly-appointed commander of the Detective Division, Capt. Leonard Hart, wasn't convinced of our theory: He thought that perhaps there'd been pressure from District Attorney Daniel J. Craig – a lifelong friend of Weir Stewart – to make something happen. While Craig was certainly concerned for his dear friend's wife, this had nothing to do with our theory, or our request to search the landfill. We were just taking the information we had, making deductions, and eliminating theories which didn't fit. Sadly, we couldn't find any component of our theory which didn't fit the facts as we then knew them. With a little help from Detectives Walden and Woods, Hart relented.

We hadn't waited for permission anyway.

Even in the winter, landfills stink. Saturday, May 14 was far from winter - the temperature reached eighty-five degrees that day. The grim search began.

With the aid of the Richmond County Sheriff's Department and the state crime lab, we used rakes to begin the painstakingly arduous and unpleasant task of sifting through piles of garbage from the area which had been pointed out by Boatright. Our crime scene tech, Duane Christenson (from whom I'd learned so much during my detective training), constructed six wooden platforms onto which a bulldozer operator would pile on the trash. There were six of us manning each of the six platforms, with only thin masks over the nose and mouth between us and the onslaught of stench. We worked throughout the morning, then took a lunch break. It wasn't the ideal environment to enjoy a meal, but there was very little about this which was enjoyable anyway.

Investigator Henry Black of the Richmond County Sheriff's Office, who was sitting next to me eating lunch, said "look at those buzzards over there. They seem to be interested in that pile of trash." I wasn't overly enthused. After all, this was a *landfill*, filled with everything from dog carcasses to medical waste. There were buzzards *everywhere*.

"When I finish my sandwich, I'm going over there to start digging," Black told me.

After lunch I left the landfill, went and got cleaned up some, and headed to Fielding's last known residence. He wasn't there. Right about this time, I heard from Investigator Kenneth Boose - working on-site at DFACS - that blood had been found on the dumpster.

I found out later that it was sometime that afternoon when Deborah Hawes, a friend of Fielding's with whom he'd been staying, noticed a Missing Person poster with Mary Colley Stewart's photo. In the photo, Mary was wearing a watch and distinctive diamond wedding ring, on which was engraved "*WWC to MMC*", the couple's initials. Hawes recognized the jewelry: Fielding had, just the previous day, given the pieces (along with another ring and some gold necklaces) to herself and another friend, Tammy Williams. Hawes had already hocked one of the rings and told Williams, "You're wearing a murder watch."

I was back out at the landfill at 5:10 p.m. that afternoon. I remember the time very well, for that's when we found Mary Colley Stewart's feet. Investigator Black's hunch about the swarming buzzards had been spot on.

We had probable cause.

When we formally charged Fielding with her murder, he said, "Y'all got me. I know you gonna fry me."

We certainly *wanted* to.

By the time the landfill search concluded on June 8th, we'd found most of Mary's body. She'd been mangled and dissected and strewn throughout the garbage heap by compactors, dozers, and excavators, and it would take a few weeks before the remains could be

One of many headlines about the case

positively identified through hair samples (prior to the lab results, the coroner could only state that the victim was "a white female fitting the height and weight of Mary Colley Stewart", and that she *might* have been strangled), but we knew it was her.

The evidence against Fielding (which we spent the next several months compiling and documenting) was overwhelming: Both his and the victim's blood had been found in various areas of the crime scene (including the canvas cart used to carry garbage bags to the dumpster), most of the victim's jewelry had been recovered from the pawn shops at which Hawes and Williams had hocked the items, and a search of Fielding's residence had turned up clothing with blood stains which matched the victim's. Additionally, the suspect had bruising, scratches, and one puncture wound on his arm, none of which had been noticed by multiple witnesses prior to Stewart's disappearance.

Finally – even though he'd plead "not guilty" – he couldn't take back his "*Y'all got me.*"

Any murder case – particularly one as horrifying and high-profile as the Mary Colley Stewart case – is an amazing feat of cooperation among scores or more of dedicated law-enforcement professionals, tirelessly piecing together an intricate puzzle with hundreds or even thousands of separate components. There's never any *single* individual who deserves full credit or full blame, yet – particularly in *our* society a single person will become the "face" of an investigation.

In this case, in my role as lead investigator, it was me. I was humbled and honored, but still wished with every fiber of my being that Mary hadn't worked late that night. That's not how life works, though. It's certainly not how death works.

At the time, I wasn't 100% sure how *anything* worked – I only knew that I'd been given a job, that I'd done it to the best of my ability, and that I'd helped catch a killer. I'd been *of service*.

I was twenty-three years old.

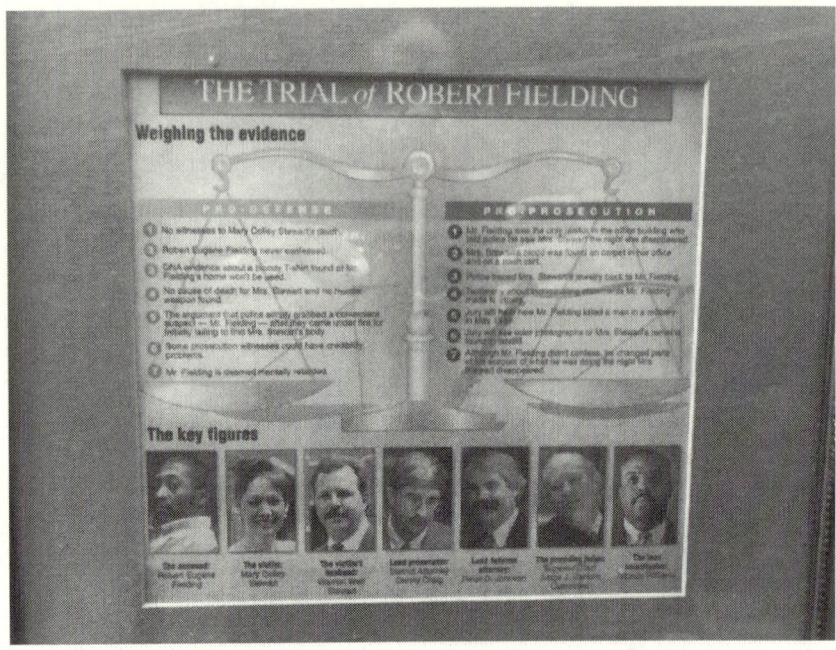

More coverage of the Mary Colley Stewart case

CHAPTER TWELVE

The Mad Mayor and

Holy Matrimony

After the Mary Colley Stewart case, I became somewhat of a "Rising Star" in the Augusta Police Department. The Police Chief at the time - Austin McLane - took a liking to me, and District Attorney Danny Craig kind of took me under his wing as we continued to work closely together building the State's case against Stewart's killer (Fielding wouldn't go to trial until September of '96 – he was convicted and sentenced to life without parole).

The Mayor, on the other hand, didn't like me so much.

Like about seventy-five percent of the APD, I was a member of the Augusta Police Officers Association, but wasn't really what you would call "active." The group had been around for some time, but hadn't really been all that active *itself*, until Mayor Charles DeVaney started making budget cuts which threatened our livelihoods. Already among the lowest-paid law enforcement officers of any metropolitan area in the state, the mayor had added insult to injury by offsetting meager pay raises with increased insurance rates, talk of furloughing some officers, and making it more and more difficult – in some cases downright impossible – to get compensated for overtime.

As the city of Augusta was dangerously close to bankruptcy, there was talk once again of consolidation with the Richmond County government, and we feared that our overtime pay was about to be lost in the shuffle. Each time we brought up the matter, we were told there just wasn't any money.

We tried to be nice about it, but were like wheels not squeaky enough to get the grease. So we squeaked a little louder.

On a Friday in February of '95, Sergeant Greg Smith (he was the president of the Officers Association) and I hand-delivered letters outlining our grievances to each and every member of the city council. If they worked, we took the letter to their office. If they didn't, we took it to their house. We did this late in the afternoon on Friday, knowing they'd have all weekend to read our complaints.

I believe the mayor started getting phone calls that night. By the next Monday morning, he was livid. He called Chief McLane, demanding to see Greg and I in his office.

"Some heads are gonna roll!" he said.

Once again, I had a sinking feeling that I'd got myself into trouble. Once again – as with the Piggly Wiggly manager and the driving course instructor – it was because I'd stood up on behalf of others.

We had about an hour and a half to get to the mayor's office, so Greg and I tried to rally 'round the troops, to get some back-up for our meeting. Our pleas fell on deaf ears.

The chief – while supportive of our cause – wasn't going to risk his career. Nor were any of the other upper-echelon officers. Everything we were doing was to benefit us *all*, but nobody was willing to stand with us and fight. It was gut-wrenching.

So I quickly developed a Plan B: if we couldn't get any of our brothers-in-arms to fight with us, we could at least gather some *witnesses*.

"I'm going to call every damned reporter in town," I told Greg.

I'd developed a good relationship with the local press – not just through the notoriety of the Stewart case, but through my community involvement, child advocacy, and mentoring. First I called Sandy Hodson of the Augusta Chronicle.

"I'll be there," she said.

Then I called each of the three TV stations in town. They showed up to City Hall as well.

Those calls may have saved our careers. They also led to getting us squeaky wheels some much-needed grease.

To say the mayor was displeased with our tactic is putting it mildly. There was a gaggle of reporters already waiting when we arrived, and Greg and I were ushered into Mayor DeVaney's office. It was reported the next day that his yelling could be heard through the thick door.

We achieved two significant things that day: The city council's Public Safety Committee agreed to form a panel to address our complaints and – thanks largely to an editorial also published the next day – we got the public on our side.

While it took some time – we wound up having to file a lawsuit on behalf of the ninety officers who were owed overtime pay – justice prevailed, and many of the shorted officers received checks ranging from five to eight thousand dollars.

Sadly, the experience also opened up my eyes to the reality that while my brothers and sisters in blue would never show any hesitation to back me up on the *street*, their courage didn't extend to matters of career. Greg and I had *both* put it all on the line for them, and they remained silent.

I'm reminded of something else my mother used to say, something I think of often when despairing about others' actions (or *in*actions) – things over which I have no control: "That's their little red wagon," she'd say. "They can push it, pull it, or flip it over."

In May of 1995, I was honored with the "Police Office of the Year" award. I'd end up getting three of those (from various civic organizations) during my tenure with the APD, and have received a total of six during my law enforcement career. While immensely gratifying and humbling, it's not the reason I got into this field – it's merely the recognition that comes from always striving to be the best I can be, and from my core belief that it's all about being *of service*.

Holding my oldest daughter Kiara at the Officer of the Year awards in Augusta

In November of 1995, I was the lead investigator in Augusta's first-known female drive-by murder. Markeza Hankerson, Lawanda Ward, and Temeka Williams were charged following the death of 14-year-old Nicole Hawes. Two of the suspects were teenagers as well. Sadly, the only thing which made this case stand out was the gender of the perpetrators. Otherwise, it was just business-as-usual, and business-as-usual was emotionally draining.

I hadn't given much thought to career advancement once I made detective – that was the dream, after all. But I've always been ambitious in my desire to be of service, and – after years of low pay, conflicts with the city government, and the disheartening realization that perhaps the APD wasn't quite the "brotherhood" I'd hoped - I knew it was time for me to move on.

Shirleta helped me make my decision: we were married on April 27th of 1996 (which was also my 25th birthday), and we had a future to build. I'd been on the same rung of my career ladder for too long, and the consolidation of the Augusta and Richmond County governments threatened to keep me planted on that rung for years to come. I wanted to take a step up, and take a step *away* from the crime and stress of the big city. I wanted to go home.

CHAPTER THIRTEEN
Broken Promises

There had been four previous referendums on consolidating the governments of Richmond County and Augusta, Georgia. It took Augusta being on the verge of bankruptcy to finally make it happen. The consolidation was approved in 1995 and went into effect in '96.

I knew pretty quickly that – as far as my career was concerned - it wasn't going to work out.

In the minds of many of us with the Augusta Police Department, the merging with the Richmond County Sheriff's Office was almost a hostile takeover. While the APD was light years ahead of the RCSO in terms of technology and training, with policies and procedures which had adapted to the increasingly-turbulent times, the county seemed to need to "assert its authority," to leave no doubt which agency was in charge. Their personnel were more entrenched as well, with advancement oftentimes more a matter of politics than merit. (As a general rule, county law enforcement agencies are more political than those of municipalities – now that I'm a sheriff, I can't say I really care for that). I realized that – instead of the rapid advancement I felt my dedication and drive warranted – it could take years, perhaps even a decade or longer, to move up.

So when Waynesboro City Councilman Dick Byne reached out to me about returning to my hometown to become the police chief, I knew it was God's plan.

As it turned out, God's plan had a few more detours and roadblocks than my own.

Byne and I met in early '96, in a secluded area of the Augusta Mall, to discuss the city council's plan to chart a new course for the city. The Georgia Bureau of Investigation (GBI) had been called in to investigate allegations of police misconduct, overseen by Special Agent in Charge Robert Ingram, with whom I'd worked closely on the Mary Colley Stewart case. He'd dropped my name to Byne.

Like many small southern towns, Waynesboro had experienced its share of racial tension. I've said before that I didn't really feel it affected *me* too much – most of the families in the projects were African-American and the schools I attended were fully segregated. I grew up *aware* of a cultural divide, but just assumed that's the way things were.

In 1984, there had been riots over the police killing of a black man while in custody. Fires were set, stores were looted, curfews were implemented and enforced. The main thing I remember about it (I would have just turned thirteen) is that Momma wouldn't let us leave the yard.

Throughout the ensuing years, there had been multiple charges of police brutality – some founded, some unfounded – leveled by members of the black community against the department. I had myself been subjected to what I considered to be racial "profiling" (a term which became part of the national vernacular following the Rodney King case): On a visit to my mother in 1992, I was pulled over for rolling through a stop sign. That I was stopped was understandable. What was *less* understandable was that the officer – known to everyone in town as

"Dirty Larry" – stepped out of his vehicle with his assault rifle. I was a patrol officer for the APD at the time, but didn't reveal that to Larry. I just asked him why he felt the need for an automatic weapon on a routine traffic stop. He explained that there were "a lot of people out to get him," and that he wasn't taking any chances. I was suspicious of that excuse, and considered calling the police chief about it, but let it slide. I figured he'd wind up getting what was coming to him. Later, "Dirty Larry" was kicked off the force for allegations of brutality and planting drug evidence. After that, he was investigated by the FBI and sent to federal prison for running a prostitution ring. So I guess I was right.

By the time Byne and I discussed the police chief job, the department was embroiled in a controversy over a black officer getting shot in the face by a white officer during a training exercise. The black officer, Corporal Marvin Jones, had survived and was suing the city. Whether it was racism or incompetence (the training exercise instructor wasn't certified and had failed to perform the most rudimentary of safety checks and firearms inspections) was never truly established, but it all contributed to the air of mistrust and hostility between the black community and the police department.

Byne and his fellow members of the Waynesboro City Council thought I might be just the guy to help re-build trust. I thought so too. The current police chief, H.L. Ivey, was planning to take a medical retirement, so the plan was for the city to hire me for the newly-created (just for me) "assistant chief of police" job, then transition me into the lead role following Ivey's retirement.

That, apparently, wasn't *God's* plan.

I accepted the position as assistant police chief in May of '96, and Shirleta and I moved into a house just down the street from my family home in Waynesboro.

The new job began on a sour note, and didn't get any better. I had to convert a janitorial closet/storage room into my office, using a six-foot folding table as a desk. I was met with thinly-veiled resentment by members of the department who had applied for the assistant chief position, unaware that it had been created specifically for me.

Waynesboro Assistant Police Chief ID

Upon Ivey's retirement, I was named "acting" chief, and immediately began *acting*: writing policies and procedures, reviewing training records, and working towards becoming a state certified agency through the Chiefs of Police Association (they had created an accreditation program for agencies who wished to follow the latest and best law enforcement practices to minimize civil liability and foster greater accountability to the public – just what Waynesboro needed). In short, I wanted to establish the same kind of trust and goodwill which I'd worked so hard to gain in the Augusta community. I wanted to be *of service*, and I wanted to make a difference.

As with the assistant police chief job, there were several applicants for the chief's job. One of those interviewed by the city council was Karl Allen, who – although spending three decades working for the Department of Corrections – had only recently become a member of the Richmond County Sheriff's Office. He hadn't even completed his FTO training yet. After his interview (the council had called an executive session to make their decision), Allen left the building. I assumed it was because he knew *I'd* be getting the job. In hindsight, I don't think that was the reason.

I was waiting patiently outside the council chambers when Mayor Martin Dolin walked through the doors, looked around, and asked loudly, "Where's our new chief?" I thought perhaps he just hadn't seen me.

"I'm right here," I said.

"No, not you."

I was crushed. I felt a level of anger, frustration, and disappointment which I think may be unrivaled in my lifetime. I simply couldn't believe that – after all I'd done to show my worthiness for a job I'd been led to believe was already *mine* – I'd be so blatantly betrayed.

They'd given the job to Allen.

Over the next few months, I heard various reasons for the city council's change of heart: that I was too young; that I didn't have a degree (had I been told that was a qualification, I never would have applied); that Waynesboro "just wasn't ready for a black police chief." I didn't believe a single one of those explanations held water or made any sense. Honestly, I think the city council just

WPD Assistant Chief Photo

lacked the courage to act in the city's best interest.

I was disheartened, disgusted, and thoroughly demoralized. I just couldn't do it. After a year with the Waynesboro PD, I resigned.

It wasn't as much "back to the drawing board" as it was "back to the grocery business."

CHAPTER FOURTEEN
Stepping Back and Stepping Up

It's often said that when God closes one door, He opens another. I've found that to be true, although I sometimes felt like some doors I slammed shut myself, and some doors I had to kick open. I've also found that some doors open and shut more quickly than others, and some doors just open onto short hallways which lead to other doors.

I was miserable as the Waynesboro assistant police chief. I'd been betrayed and publicly humiliated and felt like my hands were tied as far as trying to implement any of the changes I felt were needed to strengthen the bond between the police department and the community.

One of my patrol sergeants, Mike Godbee, had tragically lost a son in a car crash. It hit him pretty hard, and he felt like he was no longer able to fulfill some of the requirements of the job (mainly responding to vehicle crashes - a significant part of a police officer's duties). Mike was a great officer, and I was further dejected by his resignation.

He'd been hired as an assistant manager at a new "Sav-a-Lot," a low-cost grocery store chain owned by Bi-Lo. He knew about my experience at Piggly Wiggly nearly a decade earlier and mentioned to me that they were looking for a manager. And that it paid $10,000 more than what I was currently making.

It wasn't a tough choice. I needed a break. I was hired and turned in my two-week notice to Chief Allen.

People are often surprised when I tell them that being a grocery store manager was immensely more stressful than being a police officer – even in the high-crime areas to which I'd been accustomed while with the APD. When you're on the street, most of the stress comes on fast (stakeouts in dark, cold houses waiting on suspected felons notwithstanding); you react more instinctively, guided by your training. And yes, it's often a literally life-and-death stress, but it all happens so quickly that you only experience it in hindsight.

Not so with managing a grocery store. The stress of monitoring sales, finding employees who wouldn't leave you stranded for Friday-night football, and managing payroll (along with the myriad of other duties – from stocking shelves to unclogging the toilet) was a stress which was with me from the moment I opened my eyes in the morning until I closed them at night. Sometimes *sleep* wasn't even a relief, as my dreams would be ruined with the intrusion of work.

I was grateful for the leadership and financial skills I was picking up as well as for the nicer paycheck – but law enforcement was still in my blood. I'd known from the start that the Sav-a-Lot job was only temporary, and had maintained my police certification (requiring Continuing Education hours) and taught classes as an adjunct instructor at the Police Academy (by the time I left the APD, I'd been certified not only as a general instructor, but in firearms, defensive tactics, and interview/interrogations as well).

Shirleta knew the Sav-a-Lot job was temporary too, and even though she was raised by parents who had each had just one job, she understood that I belonged in law enforcement and stood by me through the job-and-house-hopping.

After I'd been denied the police chief job, I'd heard rumors that Burke County Sheriff Greg Coursey – a life-long friend of the family - had feared that I was going to use the position as a steppingstone to running for sheriff, and had used his pull to sway the city council's vote. I hadn't wanted to believe the rumors and was close enough to the sheriff that I was able to ask him about it. He denied having any hand in the decision and echoed what I'd also heard - that they'd just decided Waynesboro "wasn't ready for a black police chief." Honestly, as wrong as I thought the decision was, that explanation made the most sense.

Of course, in my righteous indignation (exacerbated by the rashness of youth), I continued to criticize Chief Allen – both privately and in letters to the editor of the local paper.

After less than a year at Sav-a-Lot, I approached Sheriff Coursey about a job. After getting my assurances that I'd take it easy on the chief and that I wasn't planning to try and take *his* job (which I found a little odd, considering what he'd told me), he created a position especially for me: I was named "Special Investigator to the Sheriff." It was the second law enforcement job in a row which had been created specifically for me. I had high hopes it would have a more satisfying outcome.

Being sworn in as Special Investigator for BCSO

It did. While by no means the pinnacle of my career, it provided – like *most* of my law enforcement jobs – experience and helped lay the building blocks of what was to come. And I felt I was once again being *of service* in a way not possible as either a grocery store manager *or* an assistant police chief. I also felt it would be a logical path to running for sheriff once Coursey retired, for although I aimed to keep my promise to not try to unseat him - *succeeding* him was now firmly on my radar. I had no idea just how far off that dream was.

Sheriff Coursey is a colorful character who on occasion referred to himself as "the High Sheriff." The first time I heard him use the term was in the early nineties: I was a detective with the APD, working an aggravated assault with intent to murder case. The suspect, Jimmy Smith, was an old friend of Sheriff Coursey's who – after we'd used the media to try to flush him out of hiding – called the sheriff to arrange a surrender in Burke County. Coursey called and told me he'd deliver Smith to us in Augusta, but that he wanted to be assured no harm would come to the suspect. "I know y'all like to shoot 'em up there," he said.

With Sheriff Coursey

When the sheriff and Smith arrived at the APD at the agreed-upon time, Investigator Tim Taylor and I met them in the bullpen (the open work area common in newsrooms and police departments). I hadn't really had time to brief Taylor on what exactly was going on, so he didn't know who this outspoken salt-and-pepper-haired man with the suspect even *was*.

He interrupted the sheriff with a "Who the hell is *this*?"

I prepared myself for Taylor's dressing-down.

"I'm the goddamned *High Sheriff*," came the reply. "Who the hell are *you*?"

Coursey then turned to me. "Where'd y'all get this little short-ass guy?"

It was difficult not to laugh at the time – now it's *impossible* not to.

Because of my experience with the APD (and, I think, in part also because his wife Susan was still the director of the Burke County DFACS), I was assigned to handle all the child abuse cases. I was also assigned internal affairs cases, which made me not just the police, but the police who *policed* the police (or, in this case, the deputies). This didn't exactly make me the most *popular* member of the department, but I'd already established a reputation as a guy who was as above-board as they come. This trait has – through the years – given me the freedom to speak out about things which *aren't* so above-board. I've always said, "If you're going to raise hell, you'd better be clean."

I also worked a couple of murder cases during my initial stint with the BCSO: One involved a woman who had shot her abusive boyfriend as he lay sleeping on the couch. She'd then buried him in the back yard and later claimed self-defense. The luminol (which, if you watch any "true crime" shows, you'll know is how crime scene investigators detect blood which may be invisible to the naked eye) said she was lying. Due to the multiple reported instances of abuse, she only got five years for the murder.

I also *witnessed* a murder. I was working a side security job at the

Mystique Lounge and had just escorted DeWayne Burke and another patron outside for fighting. Before I had a chance to react (and the parking lot bystanders would have made an armed response impossible anyway), Burke grabbed a handgun from his car and shot the other man to death, then ran into the nearby woods. We found Burke. We found the gun. He's serving life.

In my short time as a law enforcement officer, I'd seen (and investigated) tragedies on a scale which most people only read about. From child abuse to savage assaults to brutal murders, it had been my job to see that the perpetrators of these tragedies got justice. And while it was horrifying, and often made me wonder about God's plan for humanity, I'd kept it all at arm's length. I didn't let it affect me *personally*.

In 1998, the tragedy came home.

CHAPTER FIFTEEN
The Saddest Day

"Your brother Alonzo was in here earlier to buy some rope."

The statement from one of the guys who worked at the Mr. Auto Parts Napa – a store in Waynesboro where many of the local men would congregate to shoot the breeze puzzled me.

"Rope?"

"Yeah, he said he needed some rope strong enough to pull a car."

That puzzled me even *more*.

"What the hell's he need rope to pull a car for?" I asked. "Alonzo doesn't *own* a car."

It's my nature to try to make sense of the illogical. Most times, it turns out it wasn't that illogical to begin with.

"He's probably helping Miss Ada with something," I said.

Miss Ada was a black woman in her eighties who seemed a hundred. Alonzo was always helping out the old and needy folks in the community: He'd been ordained a Baptist minister (I remember his first sermon, about Jonah and the whale) and although he wasn't employed by any church (or, mostly, at *all*) – still did his best to be of service and spread God's word.

My intention was to track my twin brother down and see if he needed any help. Then I got distracted (I'd left something at the Dairy Queen after lunch that I needed to retrieve), then I got busy. It slipped my mind.

The words "If only" are among the most pointless. Hindsight is 20/20, but only serves any purpose when a lesson is learned. Usually we learn too late.

There were as many reasons Alonzo could've needed that rope as there are such late-learned lessons. Not a one of them makes any difference, and none will ever change the sad fact that, on a Thursday in August of 1998, my brother hanged himself from a tree.

Alonzo as a teenager

Alonzo and I, although fraternal twins, didn't share many similarities, neither physically nor temperamentally: Our grandfather, Lucious Sr., called us "Thunder" (me) and "Lightning" (Alonzo). He was thinner, more lightly-skinned, and studious, taking advanced classes in school while I was struggling (and – in the case of the seventh grade – *failing*) to get by. He was more of a loner, too. I remember him always taking his plate to his room, eating his meals with his nose in either a schoolbook or the Bible.

Apart from a dumpster fire he set behind the Waynesboro newspaper, *The True Citizen*, when we were ten, Alonzo didn't cause much trouble. He played football and became a bodybuilder in high school, dated and had a son – Alonzo Marquise – with the neighbors' daughter, Johnnie

Mae Evans. He also served as a firefighter and EMT with the Burke County Emergency Management Agency.

He didn't keep those jobs long. Sadly, Alonzo didn't keep *any* job long. As much as it pains me to admit it, I just thought he was lazy.

Our family is pretty blessed in the intelligence department, yet with all our smarts (all four of my sisters now have advanced degrees and there's honestly not a tool in our shed which isn't pretty sharp; I've tried my best to keep up) we were clueless about mental health issues. I always associated the concept with the "special needs" kids. I prayed for them over the cruel hand they'd been dealt and tried to be of service when I could.

We certainly didn't understand *depression*, didn't know that this wonderful brain of ours, with all its power and potential, can sometimes turn on us and make us wish we were dead. We didn't know that depression *is* a mental illness, and that about one in five will face it in their lifetime.

I think that out of all of us, Momma – the *least* educated – understood the most (although, sadly, not enough); she stood up for Alonzo when I told her she should kick him out of the house if he wasn't going to pay his fair share. I knew he'd been seeing Dr. Gilbert Banks and someone at Ogeechee Mental Health Services, but thought he was using it as an excuse – both to avoid work *and* to get medication (which he received from both). Another pointless "if only."

I'd just returned home that afternoon (Shirleta and I had bought a house in Augusta during my stint as Waynesboro assistant police chief) and was cooking dinner when I got a call on my cell phone from dispatcher Paul Gay.

"I know you just got home. But we need you back. Some guy is hanging from a tree."

So I headed back to town, Code Three (sirens, lights, high-speed).

I wasn't halfway there when Chief Deputy James Hollingsworth called me.

"Come on back to the office," he said.

Back to the office? That made no sense to me. Combined with the sudden influx of *other* calls - first from my aunt, then from my sisters (calls which, as I was driving Code Three, I left unanswered) – I started thinking *something* wasn't right. Hollingsworth wouldn't elaborate until I convinced him that I'd go "Code One" (normal speed, no lights or sirens). Then he went against protocol and told me my brother was dead.

I'm a tough guy. My upbringing required me to be tough, my job requires me to be tough. For a few moments there, alone in my car, I wasn't so tough. As I kept repeating the word "*Why??*" I was hit with the realization that – as good a damned detective as I was – I missed *so many clues*: not just the rope but the *history*, all the things which *led* to the rope. Those signs of desperation which – despite my lack of knowledge about mental health issues – I should have recognized just from spending the previous eight years of my life dealing with desperate people.

A conductor on the train which passed behind our Larry Drive home on its way into town spotted Alonzo and called 9-1-1. That was the reason the address I'd initially been given was wrong. Considering how fast those trains go, it's a wonder he saw him at all.

When I arrived at the station my sisters were there, sobbing and screaming. All those things I was no longer allowed to do. I had to be the tough guy again.

Our mother was absolutely shattered. We usually have our whole lives to prepare us to lose our parents; nothing *ever* prepares a parent to lose a child. I imagine that leaves a hole which can never be filled.

We held my brother's funeral at Rock Creek Baptist Church in Keysville (our church, Forest Hill Baptist Church, was too small to accommodate the gathering). I'll never forget the sermon, delivered by the Reverend Sylvester Nabritt, which ended with the passage from John 25:11, "And those that live in Him shall never die."

We laid Alonzo to rest in the Forest Hill cemetery, near the grandfather who'd called us Thunder and Lightning, not far from the shack and surrounding fields and woods where we'd so long ago played together, back when nothing mattered but the weather.

Back when "if only" held more hope than condemnation.

Grave Markers for Alonzo and our Grandaddy Lucious

CHAPTER SIXTEEN

A New Daughter and a Crazy Boss

I speak often of my efforts to be *of service* and set a good example, to effect a positive change in society, even if it's only one person at a time. The truth of the matter is, *all* change happens "one person at a time," because it's all up to the individual to *make* that change. If I speak to an auditorium full of high school kids, and a handful of them find inspiration in my words and are motivated to turn that inspiration into action, that handful is still made up of individuals, each inspired or motivated in a way that's uniquely personal to *them*.

All my ambition – whether to be a policeman, detective, instructor, chief, or sheriff – has been driven by the need to help, one at a time, as many people as possible. Rising through the ranks (even in the roundabout way I did) simply gave me the opportunity to reach more people, to effect change on what I hoped would be a rising and widening scale.

Obviously, there have been setbacks, and positions which were just steppingstones. But each step was a necessary part of the puzzle.

By 2000, I felt I'd reached a plateau with the Burke County Sheriff's Office. I'd promised Sheriff Coursey I wouldn't run against him, and he seemed pretty settled in (he'd wind up serving thirty-six years at the post, with a few hints at retirement during his last few terms which had us moving back and forth from Augusta to Waynesboro in anticipation of a run at the job).

Shirleta had given birth to our daughter Chandler Haley Williams on October 5th, 1999 (I called her "Stank" and "Doo-Doo" for the first few months, because it seemed all she did was eat, crap, and cry), and I felt I needed to expand my career horizons.

Columbia County (just west of Augusta) was not only significantly larger than Burke County, their sheriff's office had – in 1996 - become the first in the state of Georgia to be nationally accredited. I felt the accreditation crucial to the development of my leadership skills (as a member of an accrediting body, they had tools and resources not available to other law enforcement agencies) and that it would provide more opportunities for advancement.

With Chandler

I began work with the CCSO in 2000, spending a few months on patrol, learning the rules and procedures, before being assigned to violent crimes.

One of those violent crimes was the kidnapping, sexual assault, and murder of 17-year-old Tabitha Bosdell. While walking to her job as a telemarketer in June of that year, she was kidnapped by Reinaldo Javier Rivera, who – posing as a photographer and luring his victims to secluded areas, where he raped and strangled them - had already murdered two other young women and would go on to kill one more before he was captured and sentenced to death.

Also that month, Rodney Willingham stabbed a terminally ill cancer patient to death during a botched home invasion in search of money to buy drugs, then dumped the man's body in a well. He too was later convicted.

But it was a frustrating case where the perp went free – wasn't, in fact, even *prosecuted* – which relegated my time at CCSO to yet another steppingstone.

We had the peeping tom dead to rights: The victim, who was his next-door neighbor, positively identified him as the man who had crawled on top of her air-conditioning unit to watch through her bathroom window as she sat on the toilet. There was nothing to indicate any motive the victim may have had for concocting such a story. Who would make something like that up?

The problem was that the accused was an attorney at one of the most prestigious law firms in Augusta. A law firm with connections. As I watched my painstaking investigation become politicized, then watched as the politicians conspired to make it go away (using the time-honored tactic of assaulting the victim's credibility), I was saddened, disappointed, and disgusted. I knew it was time to move on, to yet again seek greener pastures.

That I leaked the cover-up to the media only made it easier to leave.

I spent the next year as the Assistant Director/Basic Mandate Student Coordinator at the East Georgia Regional Police Academy in Blythe.

There I assisted with day-to-day operations (things like budget and personnel) and coordinated in-services training and advanced/specialized courses. All in addition to the nine hundred hours of yearly training I prepared and instructed.

When I'd first started at the police academy a decade previously, I would most likely have laughed if you'd told me how much I'd end up *teaching* this stuff. I would have laughed even louder if you'd told me how much I'd *enjoy* it. Passing

With staff at CSRA LETC (Central Savannah River Area Law Enforcement Training Center)

on knowledge and learning is a way of being of service which can dramatically change (and *save*) lives and reap rewards through generations. There are now those I instructed who are themselves teaching. It's the gift that keeps on giving.

Unfortunately, there's more to a such a job than passing on knowledge, just as there is so much more to police and detective work than catching bad guys. As assistant director of the academy I was under director Mike Farrell, a 6'6" retired Army logistics officer.

I'm not judging – just observing and assessing based upon my own experience and well-documented facts – when I say that he was a crazy man.

He could be a great guy – he was independently wealthy (his father I believe had been a prominent doctor) - and loved to lavish money and gifts to those under his command. He bought me steak dinners almost daily. He bought steak for the Academy *dog* (her name was Judy). But there was a price to pay (well, maybe not for Judy): He frequently exhibited narcissistic, almost sociopathic behavior, and I suspected he was using his position politically in a way which was bound to get him into trouble. And I feared that, as his second-in-command, I would be tarnished from the fall-out.

Some of his behavior was relatively benign, even if bizarre: He had a thing about keeping the grounds clean. On the morning that a fresh new batch of cadets would arrive, he'd make sure all of us instructors were seen picking up litter. He did this so the new cadets would be less inclined to grumble when – shortly thereafter – he would have *them* picking up litter. One Sunday before a new class came in, I spent *hours* cleaning the grounds, just because I thought our time could be better spent – possibly *teaching*.

I'll be damned if he didn't have us picking up non-existent litter the next morning.

That was rather mild compared to "the Desk Incident."

Bill Taylor, whom I'd known since we worked together at the Augusta Police Department (he was a motorcycle Sergeant there), had been an instructor at the academy for several years. His desk was bigger than Farrell's.

Emphasis on the past tense. One day, while Bill was teaching a class, Farrell brought in a chain saw and made Bill's desk substantially smaller.

While these incidents made me seriously wonder about the mental health of the man I was working for, it was his politically-motivated behavior which I feared were going to land him – and, by association, *me* – in hot water.

Farrell was a big supporter of an extremely popular state senator – one whom he believed would be governor one day and propel him into his dream job of Director of Public Safety for the Georgia State Patrol. (He told me about his dream frequently, always adding "and you're going with me!"). We had a new cadet whom – due to his doctorate degree – Farrell assumed was somehow "connected." When Farrell told the cadet that if he wanted to pass the course, he needed to help this senator win an election, the cadet – almost in tears - reported it to me. I confronted Farrell about it (which, as you've seen, I'm rather inclined to do in such situations).

"Damnit, I'll do what I want to do. This is *my* academy," he told me.

I voiced my concerns elsewhere, was told they'd be addressed, but it was getting to the point where I was almost physically ill every Sunday with the dread of going back to work the next day.

Farrell would get fired for the incident with the cadet. The senator would eventually go to prison for unrelated transgressions.

I was long gone before *either* of those things happened.

CHAPTER SEVENTEEN

To the DA and Back

"Danny, I need a new job, and I need it *now*."

I'd reached the end of my rope at the police academy, and was confiding to my friend, District Attorney Daniel Craig (he and I had remained close since the Mary Colley Stewart case) my grave concerns regarding Farrell, and the mockery I felt he was making of the academy.

"Okay. You come work for me. You can start next week."

That's how I became an investigator for the District Attorney's Office, Augusta Judicial Circuit, and began what would become – my current job as Burke County Sheriff notwithstanding – probably the most gratifying years of my career.

Danny Craig may well be the most intelligent and inspiring person I know. He's a good, spiritual man and perhaps the brightest jurist I've ever worked with (that's saying something – I've never known *anyone* at that level of the criminal

Former DA - now Judge - Danny Craig

justice system who isn't as sharp as they come). He can quote statutes and legal precedents with the same ease with which he quotes Bible chapters and verses and can move a black audience so that you'd think he was a Caucasian Martin Luther King. He had the same effect on juries.

It was truly a joy to work for him.

When I'd started the police academy eleven years prior, I'd barely known what a district attorney *was*. Of course, I'd learned a lot in the interim (particularly working with Danny on the Stewart case), but it

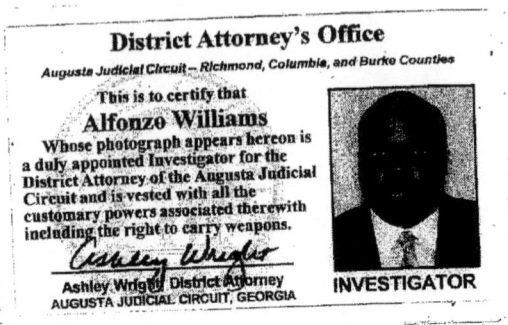

My Augusta DA Investigator's ID

was *nothing* compared to what I absorbed over the next years of assisting he and multiple other attorneys on cases brought before the Superior Court of Richmond, Burke, and Columbia counties. From interviewing witnesses of murders, rapes, and robberies to drafting indictments for child sexual abuse cases to serving as evidence custodian and providing technical assistance for courtroom presentations, I had a ringside seat (actually, it's more like I was in the corner) for multiple death penalty and many *more* felony cases.

I learned that there is no such thing as an "open and shut case." Too many variables, too much potential for legal wrangling and loophole-finding. Our job was to help the attorneys *nail* the cases shut. *Weld* them shut, if necessary. We made sure that for every piece of evidence or testimony, there were a hundred ways to back it up. If one thing was ruled inadmissible, we had equally-damning evidence waiting in the wings.

The police and detectives are charged with getting criminals off the streets. It was our job to help *keep* them off.

It wasn't just the work which was so gratifying, the new-found familiarity with all the nuts and bolts of the criminal justice system (I frequently used terms such as *in absentia, amicus, inculpatory* and *exculpatory, motion in limine,* and *writ of certiorari* – and knew what the hell they *meant*); it was also the environment outside the courtroom, back in the office – the spirit of good-natured camaraderie of the majority of those who worked in the DA's office. And Danny led the way there as well, throwing pizza parties and – on a whim – declaring a cheesecake bake-off.

"Who likes to make cheesecake?" he'd ask.

Pound Cakes

I brought pound cake pretty much every week. It's easy to get the impression from my story that baking pound cakes is a means of trying to offer comfort or consolation. Often, in my family, it is. But sometimes it's just 'cause folks like pound cake. And I've got it down. I put the recipe at the end of the book, so that no matter what you think of my story, it'll still have a happy ending.

My time with Danny and the DA's office came to a happy – or at least amicable – ending a couple of different times.

Throughout my career - beginning in the late nineties - I've worked on furthering my education, and have earned five degrees now, all done in my spare time. In my case, I credit hard work more than "book smarts." As I've mentioned, my *sisters* got all that. During my first years with the DA, I had been working on a Bachelor of Science degree in Organizational Management, and – in May of 2005 – received my degree from Voorhees College. After Mike Farrell was fired from the Police Academy in 2002, I'd been told that if I had a four-year degree and ever wanted to take the reins as Academy Director, I should look them up.

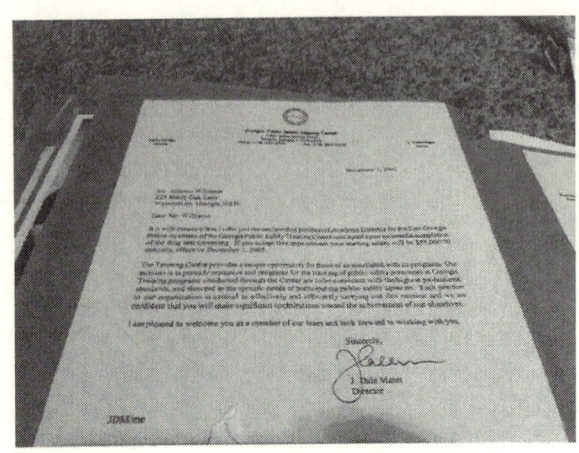
GPSTC letter of Promotion to Director 2005

So I did. And I was hired. The only problem I'd ever really had with the academy was Farrell, and I felt that - as director - I had an opportunity to really make a difference, to effect a change. To be of service.

I thought wrong.

Politics is everywhere, in almost every facet of our working and social lives. I've never cared for it much, as I've often found myself getting the short end of the stick. Of course, I'm sheriff now – about *the* most political of law enforcement jobs, at least on the county level - and it may seem somewhat disingenuous of me to bemoan the nature of the beast which played a large role in getting me here.

It doesn't mean I have to like it.

As assistant director of the academy, the politics was more overt and came in the form of actual corruption. As director, the politics was more subdued, more in line with the kind which we *all* face, no matter what our job.

The guy directly under me and the guy directly *over* me were golf buddies. If I made a decision or wanted to implement a change that my assistant director didn't like, he'd just tell the *regional* director about it on the golf course. The chain of command skipped a link. I also felt hampered by some of those who had stayed at the academy after I left and were now resentful that I'd been given the job they thought *they* deserved.

Once again, I'd started a job with the highest of hopes, only to have them dashed by elements beyond my control.

I was welcomed back to the DA's office with open arms in 2006. That Thanksgiving, we lost my brother Homer.

Homer was the oldest of us kids, born in 1962, and had a heart of gold. He was pretty much the "man of the house" as we were growing up, helping our mother keep us in line, helping us with our homework. Whether it was math or throwing a football or playing ping-pong, Homer was an expert instructor, and taught us with love and perfection. He'd married his high-school sweetheart, Glenn Jones (our neighbor from the projects), and together they'd had three children, one of whom had died shortly after birth. He was a truck driver and one of the best checkers players I've ever known.

Homer had been diagnosed ten years earlier with sarcoidosis, an inflammatory disease that usually affects the lungs and lymph glands. There is no cure – sometimes it goes away on its own, but usually it kills you in ten years. Homer, in his job as a truck driver, was a master of schedules. He could tell you precisely how long it would take to get from Point A to Point B. Sadly, as far as his sarcoidosis diagnosis went, he was right on schedule. He was less than a week from his 44th birthday.

As I'd done following Alonzo's death eight years prior, I taught a class the next day. Some may think that callous, some may try to analyze me and surmise that's just my way of dealing. I don't think about the "why" so much. I just know that life goes on, until it doesn't.

Homer's first car. We each purchased "old-people" cars as our first vehicles because our Uncle Lucious helped us.

Politics once again reared its ugly head toward the end of my second stint with the DA's office, but it was a bit more hateful this time. It was 2008, so you probably already know where I'm going with this.

As a life-long Democrat – and, of course, a life-long African-American – I was (and still am) a big Obama

fan. Many in the Augusta DA's office were not. I witnessed first-hand the kind of divisiveness, based less on issues than along deep-seeded cultural lines, which we've since seen tear our country apart.

I probably could have lived with that. I told myself many times that it wasn't my job to fight Obama's battles. I also could have lived with having a new boss, Ashley Wright, who became DA after Danny became a judge. I'd helped Ashley (who's also a judge now) on many cases over the years. She was also smart as a whip, hard-working, and always professional.

Still, it was nothing like working for my old friend.

These were only slightly mitigating factors in my decision to leave. The overriding reason was opportunity.

My friend Ken Jones called me up one day and said he was writing a program for a new police academy at Augusta Technical College. He asked if I wanted to sign on as their lead instructor.

Named "the Peace Officers Training Academy," the eighteen-week course Ken and I got up and running was a departure from the state-run academy in that – rather than training those who'd already been hired as law-enforcement officers – we taught those who aspired to be in law-enforcement. As it was under the auspices of the college, there was initially a preconceived notion that the course was more academic than hands-on. My experience and training went a long way to overcome that stigma.

Because we weren't part of a state agency, the atmosphere was much less politically charged, and minus many of the bureaucratic headaches which had plagued me during my previous teaching jobs. I loved it, and stayed with them for three years. The Peace Officers Training Academy is still going strong today.

In 2011, my hometown came calling again. They wanted me to be the new Waynesboro Police Chief. This time – almost exactly fifteen years after they'd lured me there with the same promise – they assured me they meant it.

CHAPTER EIGHTEEN
Hometown Chief

In 1996 - when I'd gone through the heartbreak and disappointment of being offered the job of Waynesboro Chief of Police, only to have the city council change their minds – it had been rumored that I only wanted the job as a steppingstone to becoming Burke County Sheriff.

Until then, I hadn't really even thought about it. When Sheriff Coursey hired me two years later as a special investigator for the county and made me promise not to run against him, I was thinking about it a *little* – but not so much that I had any trouble making - and keeping - that promise.

By the time the city offered me the job as police chief in 2011, there was no doubt in *anyone's* mind that I'd be running for sheriff. I couldn't have hidden it if I tried.

My friend Richard Roundtree (now Richmond County Sheriff) and I had discussed running for the office in our respective counties many times. We were both African-American Democrats and President Obama was still riding a wave of popularity, so we believed there had never been a better time to go for it. I'd moved my family back to Burke County in 2010 specifically to establish residency there two years before running, as the law required. Coursey hadn't declared his retirement (and my promise to him still held), but he'd hinted at it enough to warrant re-locating. Of course, he'd hinted before, and I'd moved before, but he'd been in the position over thirty years by this point and it seemed retirement was looming on the horizon.

Roundtree won his election and became sheriff of Richmond County. I accidentally became Waynesboro Police Chief.

I'd harbored no ambitions for the job when I moved back – I was just positioning myself to run for sheriff. In the meantime, I was happy being of service at Augusta Technical College and was proud of the work Ken Jones and I were doing with the Peace Officers Training Academy there. But it turned out my hometown *needed* me. Karl Allen (who'd remained on the job since '96) was embroiled in controversy, with several of his officers accused of abuse and sexual harassment; crime was bordering on what could be called *rampant*, and there hadn't been as much distrust between the community and the police since the riots of the eighties. I thought my city deserved better.

I wasn't the only one. The vice-mayor, James Jones, had told a local TV station that he was "embarrassed," and the city council in September of 2010 had come just one vote shy of firing Allen. Things hadn't improved.

We lived in the Academy Avenue section of town, and several members of the neighborhood association and I went to the city council and requested a "vote of no confidence" in Chief Allen. The council had finally had enough, the city itself had had enough, and I guess Chief Allen had too. He retired in early 2011.

Although I'd only moved back to Waynesboro with a run for sheriff in mind – and firmly believed that I could've stayed with Augusta Tech and still been a good position to get elected in 2012 – I knew that there wasn't anyone better suited to take over as police chief. And I kind of felt it was my duty. So I took a pay cut and took the job.

And got right to work.

After just a few months, the Augusta Chronicle wrote that I was "kicking butt and taking names." The department I inherited *needed* some butt-kicking and name-taking: training was poor, turnover was high, morale was low, and citizens complained that they never even *saw* the police in their neighborhoods unless they were coming to pick somebody up. It had seemed that the WPD was neither serving *nor* protecting.

Article from the Waynesboro True Citizen

As well-equipped as I was to tackle training issues (by this time I'd been an instructor in almost every aspect of policing for quite a few years) and step up our crime-fighting efforts (we doubled our presence on the streets, got computers in our patrol vehicles, and created specialized narcotics, gambling, and gang units), I felt that my number-one mission was to re-establish *trust* with the community. I've said that I'm more the "social worker" type of law enforcement officer, with the core belief that our jobs are more about helping people than simply catching the bad guys. Now – for the first time in my career – I was in a position where I could *really* do something about that.

My goal as police chief was – as with all my law-enforcement jobs - to more effectively fight crime; but *fighting* crime means the law has already been broken. I've always felt that agencies such as police and sheriff's departments have the opportunity and the resources to be agents of change in helping to create an environment where fewer laws are broken in the first place.

With this in mind, we created the first-ever Community Services Division within the department. We got inmates from the Burke County Sheriff's Office to paint and fix up bicycles from the evidence locker, which we distributed to low-income families. We had cookouts in the projects. We teamed up with the Optimists Club. For every arrest we made (and we made plenty), we spent many more hours trying to make it so we didn't *have* to arrest so many.

Two *True Citizen* articles from my first year as Waynesboro Police Chief

We made the community feel like the WPD was *their* police department. Because it was. We started a 15-member review team which acted as an advisory committee, comprised of community members from all walks of life – from banking and industry to clergy and small-business owners – and met with them regularly, me appraising them of developments within the department, they voicing their questions and concerns.

Our efforts weren't without controversy: There was some grumbling when we arrested over a dozen black juveniles who'd been committing burglaries and robberies that we were "locking up all our black kids." As the first African-American police chief in Waynesboro, I was hurt a little by the underlying accusation, but – as I mentioned before – that's the kind of thing which has followed me throughout my career. I imagine it's the same for *every* officer of color.

There were also folks who weren't too happy with some of the "house-cleaning" I did: I brought in some outside help (those who didn't know everyone in town) in an effort to alleviate the mistrust which had sprung from what was perceived as a "good ole boy" environment.

We started a Citizens Police Academy, an Explorers program (for 12-18 year-olds who thought they might want a career in law enforcement), and

Waynesboro Chief of Police

a *COPS* (Citizens on Patrol) program, the latter where we trained civilians in law-enforcement basics, taught them how to use the radio and what to look out for, and sent them out on patrol in white cars with amber police lights. We didn't give them the authority to make arrests, we didn't give them weapons. They were more like mobile "Neighborhood Watch" units than anything, although one of our COP members – a man in his seventies – did tackle and restrain a felon on the front lawn of a home the man had just burglarized. We gave the elderly gentleman, a Mr. Brozagini (now deceased), an award for his heroism, but let it be known that we didn't condone such actions.

The community for the most part loved the program, and it did my heart good to wake up in the middle night to go to the bathroom and see one of those white cars, its amber light flashing, driving slowly through the neighborhood. But it had its detractors.

I got a call one day from Frank Rotondo, who was the director of the Georgia Association of Chiefs of Police.

"Tell me it's not true, Alfonzo," he said in his thick New York accent. "I hear you've got civilians riding around in police cars, doing police work."

This pissed me off a little.

"First of all, you're not my boss," I told him. "Secondly, I don't appreciate your accusatory tone when you don't know what the hell you're talking about."

I went on to explain the program to him, to dispel those preconceived notions he'd chosen to rely on before he had all the facts.

He eventually lauded the "brilliance and creativity" of the program in a letter published in Police Chief Magazine.

And there was concern that we were going to "break the city" with the new programs and initiatives. Most of those concerned were, like Frank Redondo, not aware of the facts: Those who complained about the $36,000 price tag for the new computer system which put laptops in every police car conveniently ignored that the cost was to be covered with a fee added to municipal court convictions and traffic citations; those who wondered how we could afford to have twelve to fifteen officers patrolling our five-and-a-half-square-mile city on Friday and Saturday nights were unaware that most of the extra help was unpaid cadets I'd been teaching at the Academy.

Despite the doubters and naysayers, crime was cut drastically and trust had been restored. Overall, the town hadn't been so happy with its police in years. It was very gratifying.

In 2012, Sheriff Coursey announced that he wasn't quite ready to retire, and that he'd be seeking re-election. I was greatly disappointed, but I can't say I was all that *surprised*. I started to think that maybe it wasn't in the cards. Maybe I'd misread God's plan (as we're likely to do).

Never one to rest on my laurels, I started looking for more and better opportunities to be of service. I've always been proud of my record of working with juveniles, whether investigating cases of abuse or mentoring, so I briefly considered an offer to head up the Augusta Youth Development Center. It meant a significant raise and a chance to help some really troubled youth, but I backed out at the last minute: Directors at the YDC had a tendency to not last too long, and I was looking – finally – for a job I might be able to one day retire from.

That I'd even *entertained* the offer set some tongues to wagging among the Waynesboro powers-that-be, which reminded me again of my distaste for small-town politics. When I was offered the job of police chief of the Richmond County School System – and the opportunity to serve as top law enforcement officer over 32,000 students and 4500 employees – I couldn't turn it down. I was truly touched by the outpouring from the community and the petitions which were circulated to try to keep me in Waynesboro, but I felt I'd made a contribution and initiated changes which would continue to benefit my hometown long after I'd gone.

If I'd known how wrong I was, I probably would have stayed.

CHAPTER NINETEEN
Getting Ready to Run

In March of 2013, when I took over as police chief for the Richmond County School System, the horror of Sandy Hook – the December 2012 mass school shooting which left twenty kids dead – was still fresh on people's minds. As a law enforcement officer who'd spent the bulk of his career working with youth, and as the father of a school-age child (my youngest daughter Chandler was thirteen), I took it personally.

As a boy growing up in Burke County, schools were a refuge from the streets, a place where the worst thing that could happen would be a tussle with a playground bully or a paddling from a teacher. The good ole days. I never would have dreamed there would come a time when many public schools would include metal detectors in their budgets.

Richmond County Board of Education Police Chief ID

Our schools were becoming as dangerous as the streets. In some cases, more dangerous. As I'd made a difference in Waynesboro, so too, I believed, could I make a difference in the schools. As I told Tracey

McManus of the Augusta Chronicle in an interview held before I left Waynesboro, "If we're going to resolve crime and poverty and homelessness and delinquency and abuse, we've got to start with our children." I felt this job was not only an opportunity to be of service and a role model to a vulnerable population, but that it was a job which offered security for my family and a nice retirement.

I thought, after all these years, that *this* was God's plan.

I speak often about God's plan. One can read my story, or my resume, and think that perhaps His plan was rather haphazard in my case, that surely He didn't intend for me to get where I am today by such a *circuitous* route. But that's the thing about God's plan: It's *His*. It doesn't matter what *we* think it is. Most times, we think wrong.

I thought wrong again.

During my nearly four years of service with RCSS, I gave it my all. I wasn't just responsible for the day-to-day operations of the school safety and security department, I also performed pre-employment background checks, prepared reports for the deputy school superintendent, investigated parent and citizen complaints, and gave lectures on school emergency preparedness, school shootings, gangs, cyberbullying, and other school safety-related topics.

And I drove the bus. Pretty much every day there would be bus drivers calling in, so I was up at 5:30 each morning to pick up kids before I traded in the bus for my patrol car. Then I'd drive the bus in the afternoon. My Uncle Lucious, Jr. and my father had both been school bus drivers, and I still had fond memories of the "#65" from my childhood, so it wasn't a responsibility I complained about too much.

As a long-time investigator of crimes against children, I was hyper-vigilant of inappropriate behavior by teachers toward students: I just wouldn't put up with it. Six teachers resigned during my first year at RCSS (when told by the school system's HR Director, Norman Hill, that I didn't have the power to fire teachers, I told him I *hadn't* – they quit. He didn't say anything else about it).

As happy as I was with the work, as proud as I was of the bond I'd developed with the students and of the fact that during my tenure there had only been a single firearms-related incident (an elementary school student brought a gun to school and was playing with it at his desk when it discharged, causing a minor injury to another student), I once again felt trapped in a job where my hands were tied by politics: All major policy decisions were left to the superintendent and the school board. That frustration was compounded by the guilt I felt over having miscalculated the direction of the Waynesboro Police Department upon my departure. I thought I'd left things in good hands with my deputy chief, Roosevelt Lodge. I'd thought wrong. Within two months the city had brought in Augustus Palmer, III from Atlanta (Lodge was fired that September). Within six months, Palmer had dismantled most of the community service programs I'd started: crime was back up (more than doubling in some cases), morale and community trust back down. The city's law enforcement went to hell in a hand basket. Of course I felt somewhat responsible.

As the dream of a long career with RCSS flickered and faded, the dream of being Burke County Sheriff was reignited. When - on January 14th, 2016 - Gregory Coursey announced he was retiring after thirty-six years, it became an inferno.

CHAPTER TWENTY
Politicking

For most of my career I've looked at politics in a negative light, my perception tainted not just by the inner political machinations which have often played a role in career aggravation, but the divisiveness of politics on a national scale, often along racial lines.

That's why I find it wonderfully encouraging and inspiring that without the friendship, help, and guidance of a white conservative Republican, I never would have become Burke County's first black sheriff. Who's also a Democrat (albeit a *conservative* one).

Lewis Blanchard and I, despite our differences, are pretty much cut from the same cloth: our lives have both been based on a desire to serve, and we both view law enforcement as a calling. We've just taken different paths along the way.

With Lewis Blanchard

Raised in a middle-class family in Evans, Georgia, Lewis – like myself – grew up dreaming of being a policeman. He moved to Hilton Head, South Carolina after high school and spent six years on Beach Patrol, returning to his home state in 1989 to become Director of Campus Police & Public Safety for the Columbia County School System. In 1994, he'd been named "Police Officer of the Year" for saving the lives of two high school students.

In 1998, Lewis left law enforcement to pursue a business dream, taking "being of service" to a different and more literal realm: He started *Executive Marketing Service*, a hospitality company catering to premier sporting events – most notably the legendary Augusta Masters Golf Tournament, with which EMS has had a working relationship for many years.

After building up his company (and purchasing several restaurants and bars), Lewis was once again drawn to the law, and in 2010 he became a Lieutenant with the Taliaferro County Sheriff's Office, working part-time while still operating his business (which thrives to this day). In 2013 he went to the Richmond County Sheriff's Office, again as a Lieutenant.

Along the way, he gained valuable experience working in politics – he ran for Columbia County sheriff in 2004, then in 2012 managed the campaign of Scott Peebles, who was running against Richard Roundtree for sheriff of Richmond County (I supported Peebles, who was interested in making me his chief deputy; Roundtree never forgave me). Although neither of those campaigns were successful - Peebles took Roundtree to a run-off and lost by just over four hundred votes - Lewis learned how campaigns *worked*, and in 2014 asked me if I'd considered running for Burke County sheriff in 2016. I told him "considered" probably wasn't a strong enough word for it. He wasn't volunteering to be my campaign manager – he was applying two years in advance for the chief deputy job.

When Coursey announced in January of 2016 that he wouldn't be running for re-election that November, Lewis and I started having weekly meetings at "Somewhere in Augusta," a restaurant/bar he had purchased, made a success, then sold, strategizing about my political debut. I told him that yes, of course, he could be my chief deputy – he was as qualified as they come – as he taught me all about "politicking": organizing, time management, and, most importantly, asking for money (something I'd *never* been comfortable doing).

Proverbs 27:17 says that "Iron sharpens iron." I think my friendship and working relationship with Lewis is as fine an example of that as you'll find. What had been just a dream for so long was quickly becoming something I had confidence could become *real*.

Although unfamiliar with Burke County specifically, Lewis knew business and he knew politics, and guided me through organizing the campaign. He acted as treasurer; Crystal Phinazee Preston and her mother Jeanette Preston (two wonderful, bright, and hard-working women whose family has – for a century now – operated a local funeral parlor) acted as campaign manager and assistant campaign manager, respectively.

I think it's safe to say that Burke County had never seen as well-organized a campaign as our efforts in the summer and fall of 2016. Sheriff Coursey had predicted we'd be able to raise $10,000 from the local townspeople – we did *way* better than that. We rented office space for our campaign headquarters, put up billboards and yard signs, had barbecue dinners every Saturday, held clergy breakfasts, business breakfasts, farm meetings, retired teachers' meetings, and formal galas.

Although I had been inundated with requests – often *pleading* - to come back to law enforcement in Burke County from the time I'd left the Waynesboro Police Chief job (one city council member actually showed up at the Richmond County School Board meeting where I was confirmed as RCSS chief, begging them not to give me the job – "*we* need him," she'd said), and even though I had Sheriff Coursey's endorsement, my election was far from a "done deal." Many

Filling out paperwork to run for Sheriff

in the county had serious doubts. Some thought I was going to be a sheriff for the black community. Others thought I'd be a sheriff for the *white* community. Still others were convinced I was a typical "tax-and-spend liberal," and that I'd break the budget (one farmer told me during the campaign, "We know you'd make a damned good sheriff. We're just not sure we can *afford* you." I told him they couldn't afford *not* to have me).

With a young campaign supporter

Of course, I wasn't going to

break the county, and I certainly wasn't going to be a sheriff who served a single demographic; but it's much tougher to convince people they've been misled than it is to mislead them in the first place.

My Republican opponent in the race was Freddie Yelton, who had been a local business owner up until he joined the WPD in 2013. Apart from a failed challenge to my residency, it was a race with mutual respect and no mudslinging to speak of.

Some of my greatest support came from the unlikeliest of places: During the campaign, I became friends with Ryan Mobley, a young white farmer from Girard, Georgia (in Burke County). He had immense enthusiasm and confidence in me and shared that with his entire family – including his father Grady, a well-known-and-liked businessman and farmer. The goodwill they developed for me in the county, the hearts and minds they turned in my favor, is not something all the billboards and yard signs in the world could have accomplished. Ryan has remained a good friend, and a friend of the Sheriff's Office, often catering community events from his *Fish Eye Grill* restaurant.

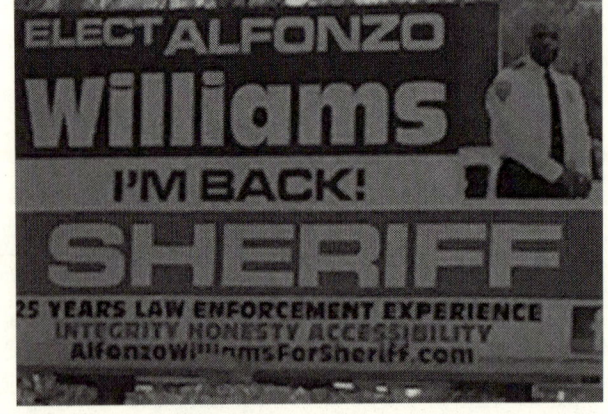

Election Day – on November 8, 2016 – was beautiful, with clear skies and a high which nearly hit seventy degrees. Although by this time we were pretty confident in the outcome (we'd actually bought a billboard proclaiming – a la "Poltergeist" – *I'm Back!*), we didn't let up. We hired fifty people, mostly teenagers and folks who just needed the work, to stand near the polling stations and at major intersections holding signs, we gave rides (regardless of political affiliation) to the polls, we provided snacks and drinks to those waiting in line.

That night we rented out the Liberty Market directly across the street from our campaign headquarters, decorated it with red, white, and blue bunting and balloons, and served refreshments to our friends, families, and supporters as the election results rolled in.

It wasn't even close.

My wife Shirleta and daughter Chandler on Election Night

As the local news announced that I'd been elected with 72% of the vote, I thought about the long road here; I thought of the dreams of a young boy and the plans of a young man; I thought of all the roadblocks and frustration which had hounded me over the nearly twenty years since I'd told Sheriff Coursey

A Proud Moment

that, once he retired, I wanted his job. I thought of the times I'd almost given up.

I thought of my late brothers, Alonzo and Homer, and how proud they would have been. I hugged my family and kissed my wife.

The next day, I got busy.

Our Mother and her remaining children

CHAPTER TWENTY-ONE
Working the Dream

"You're asking for *how* much?"

There were close to forty of us in "Sheriff's School" - held at the Georgia Public Safety Training Center in Forsyth shortly after the election - and if they'd held a vote for "Most Likely to Be a One-Term Sheriff," I

Alfonzo Williams to be sworn in as first African American sheriff in Burke County

would've won *that* by a much wider margin than my 72% Burke County victory. They thought I was crazy, and they weren't the only ones.

Change ain't cheap. I knew what needed to be done, and Lewis and I had been working out the numbers throughout the spring and summer, using Sheriff Coursey's budget as our starting point.

We needed an additional $838,000.

It wasn't just the patrol cars which had 300,000 miles on them, or the antiquated, ineffective radio system (it wasn't uncommon for a deputy to not even be able to *reach* dispatch from certain parts of the county);

it wasn't just that – in order to eliminate reliance on neighboring counties - we needed our own SWAT team and narcotics division; it wasn't just that we had jailers making $11.50 an hour and road patrolmen making $13.50 an hour (we literally had officers on public assistance).

It was more that crime was back through the roof (the years since I'd left the police chief job in Waynesboro had seen a steady increase in crime county-wide – some categories, like larceny, had more than *doubled*); we needed more boots on the ground and butts in the cars.

When I was elected sheriff, the department had four officers assigned to each shift – a sergeant, a corporal, and two deputies. That's *it*. Burke County covers 835 square miles, the second-largest county by area in the state. Whereas, in Augusta, a "1078" call (officer needs help) would result in back-up within two or three minutes, the waiting time in Burke County could often be a half hour or longer.

That wasn't going to cut it. By far, the biggest part of the budget we proposed was going toward hiring new officers. And we wanted to bring in the *best*.

I knew right where to find them.

I've said that my old friend Richard Roundtree had become considerably less friendly toward me when I supported his challenger in the 2012 Richmond County sheriff's race. I daresay I only added fuel to *that* fire when I took thirty of his deputies.

Thirty. Approximately the same number as the miles from which his yelling could be heard when he found out. That's just a guess.

We weren't offering them raises: They would be hired at about the same salaries (but with stipends added for K-9 and SWAT duties), and they'd be required to undergo three times the amount of training they were used to. They were there for better leadership. Better training opportunities. More value and respect from an administration that cared. Better promotional opportunities. To enjoy a community who gave them the same value and respect.

Although we were requesting an unprecedented budget (or, rather, an *amendment* to the budget already passed that September), we thought we had figured out a way to get it approved by the county commission with the least amount of grief possible – we'd get Sheriff Coursey to go along with us to the meeting. Lewis and I went to Coursey, told him what we were asking for and why, and asked if he might not want to speak to the commission members and not only smooth the transition, but leave office knowing he'd just given nice raises to the staff. He declined. It was worth a shot.

When I talk to students and cadets about goal setting and making plans, I always tell them to have a back-up. And a back-up to the back-up. Then another back-up to *that*. There are too many unknown variables to ever put all your eggs in one basket.

Plan B took decidedly more politicking.

The commissioners knew how much we were asking for – my letter to County Administrator Merv Waldrop had been well-publicized - and several of the commissioners (particularly chairman Wayne Crockett) were a country mile from being convinced. Lewis and I, along with the Mobleys, met face-to-face with each of the commissioners (apart from Crockett) during the week – Lewis and the Mobleys with the white members, I with the blacks. That may sound cynical to some, but it's simply a political reality in the South.

On the night of the county commission meeting, I spoke for over an hour. I told the commissioners in precise detail why we needed every bit of what we were asking for, reminding them again that the changes I'd made as police chief had raised lots of eyebrows too, but that they'd been extremely effective in bringing down the crime rate and raising the level of trust between law enforcement and the community.

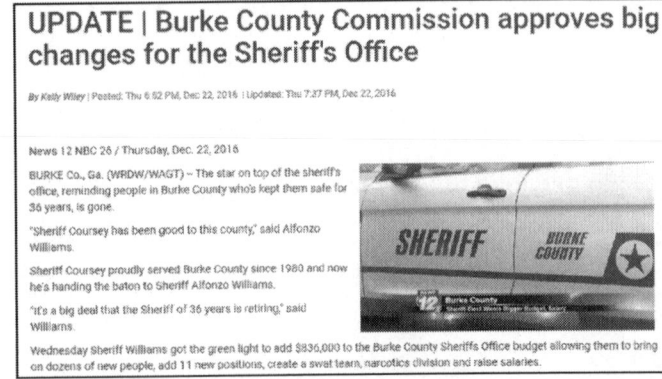

I simply wanted to make those changes county-wide now.

I also asked for more money for myself. It really had nothing to do with the salary itself (I was taking a pay cut from my RCSS job regardless); it was the principle. The salary prescribed for the sheriff's job by the state is the same amount – about $65,000 - my opponent would have started at. My opponent only had

Dreams CAN come true!

three years' experience. I had over a quarter century of experience and two master's degrees (I'm working on my third). I deserved more, and I was willing to do more work – adding animal services and code enforcement to my duties – to justify it.

In the end, I accepted less money than I'd requested for myself (although still a nice bump from that set by the state). But we got everything else.

I was sworn in at the Burke County Courthouse on the morning of December 20th. On New Year's Day, 2017, we started serving the county. True to my word, we added thirty officers to our ranks on that day.

I'd been publicizing my plans for the first hundred days in office. They were ambitious plans, and we exceeded them. We were rebuilding the sheriff's office from the ground up, and this entailed everything from painting walls and ripping up carpet to trading in our old weapons for new Glocks to meeting with EMA Chief Rusty Sanders about the radio system to organizing the first county-wide Easter egg hunt. And more. A *lot* more.

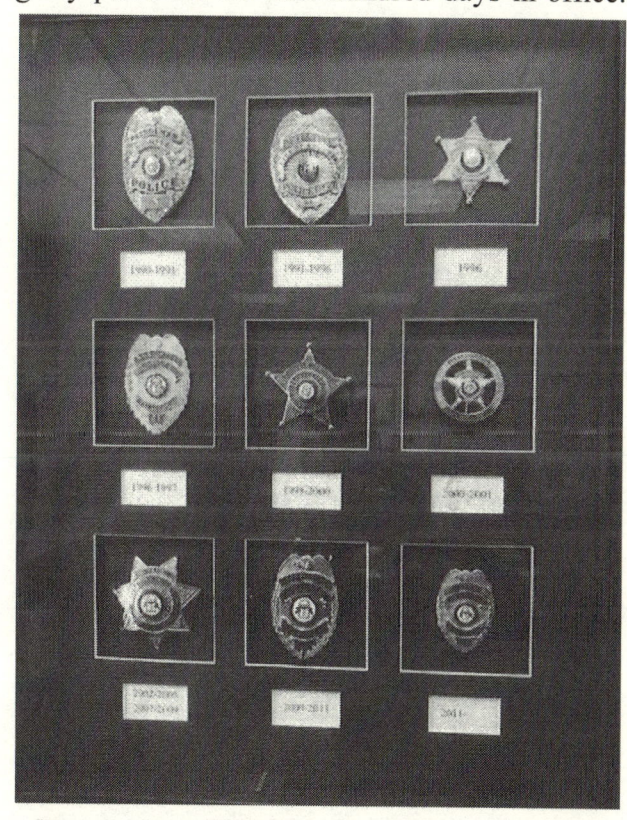

Some of the badges I've been honored to wear

The Community Services Division I'd formed as police chief (which had been a roaring success, only to be dismantled by my successor in 2013) was re-formed under the auspices of the Sheriff's Department. The Citizens Police Academy was back, the Youth Explorers Program was back. We started new programs as well, including the Senior C.A.R.E. (Caring About Resident Elderly) Program and Camp Impact (mentoring troubled young men aged 12-16).

We also created an interactive website (BurkeCountySheriff.com) and started a Facebook page (we now have nearly 18,000 followers). All in the interest of being *of service.*

In our first year and a half on the job, crime dropped 52% across the board. During our first term, we never once went over budget. And there's not a sheriff's office within a hundred miles of here that is as involved with the community.

In October of 2017, Christopher Grubisa was a healthy electrician with a wife and three kids. He thought he was getting the flu, started feeling worse and worse, and eventually went to the hospital. He was unaware that he'd contracted a rare form of bacterial meningitis – two days later, he was a quadruple amputee.

The Burke County Sheriff's Office began a campaign to build Christopher and his family a new home. We started a GoFundMe page, got contractors to donate their time, and built the Grubisas a $300,000 house, with all the features and amenities necessary for his catastrophic condition. That's the kind of thing you won't find in any law enforcement how-to book anywhere.

Nothing I've ever done in my career has been so fulfilling and rewarding as my first term as Burke County Sheriff and - as far as I can tell - the only folks here who aren't happy with the job we're doing are the criminals.

"The Son of Man came not to be served but to serve." That's from Matthew 20:28 and, as I mentioned at the beginning, is the Scripture I live my life by.

It's been nearly fifty years since Alonzo and I played together on the trash heap outside our dilapidated wooden house in Keysville; over forty years since we moved to the home in the projects here in Waynesboro. Thirty years since I first pinned on a badge. There's not been a minute of it that was exactly what you'd call "smooth sailing" and - apart from the losses of those who left far too early - there's not a minute of it I'd change for anything. Every misstep has been a lesson in life, every success a lesson in humility, and every twist in the road a reminder that we're all just along for the ride.

None of us knows what tomorrow brings, except that one day our time on earth will be over. If I die tomorrow, or if – when the next election rolls around – the citizens of Burke County decide they want a new sheriff, I won't shed a tear. I've lived a life of untold blessings, with memories of love and laughter and friendship which can never be undone.

Badges 2011 - present

And no matter what happens, I'll know without a doubt that it'll be enough to say Grace over.

ACKOWLEDGEMENTS

Thank you so much for reading *Not Here to Be Served*. I feel like I have been preparing for this very moment for a lifetime. I did not know what it would look like or when I could put a name to it, but I know it always felt right. Matthew 20:28 declares, "just as the Son of Man did not come to be served, but to serve…" I've always felt this was my calling.

For years, I had a desire to write a book about a life that would memorialize the difficulties, good and bad, twists and turns. To write about those who grew up with me, left me early and who made me better.

I had a few inspirations over the years from professors, motivational speakers, and friends who would encourage me to "just start writing." When I finally decided to do so, I wrote 20,000 words over the course of a few weeks. Then began the work of thoroughly sifting through the minds of those whose memories were more vivid than mine.

My story has not been nearly as cohesive as it appears in this book. So many more stories, case investigations, friendships, hardships, and lessons learned could have been shared. Writing this book has afforded me the opportunity to address regrets, hopefully make some amends, and – most importantly - to thank my mother, Rosa Lee Williams for giving me life, discipline, wisdom and understanding. Above all, as she would say, for raising me "under the admonition of the Lord."

This is my first book. But, certainly not my last one. I am already working on a book about a murder case I worked in Augusta, Georgia surrounding the kidnapping and subsequent murder of a social worker.

Writing is harder than I thought and more rewarding than I could have ever imagined. None of this would have been possible without my wife, Shirleta. She has always been supportive, even when my decisions may not have been the best. Her commitment to family and God is incomparable to any struggles I put us through.

I am eternally grateful to my sisters (Dr. Angela Williams, Teresa Cobb, Cassandra Williams, and Jennifer Williams), who have so much trust and confidence in me to do what is right. They have taught me discipline, tough love, manners, respect, and so much more that has helped me succeed in life. I truly have no idea where I would be if we were not as close as we are. All the family dinners, group chats, and tough love made this possible. Thank you Alice and Willie Flint for being very fine in-laws.

To Kiara and Chandler, my amazing daughters who perhaps think I am the greatest of all time (at least sometimes). You have been beautiful children and have brought me incomparable joy. I am not sure I always made the best decisions, but I always had your best interests at heart. Both of you are beautiful and respectful people and that is enough to say grace over!

My aunt Lula Mae Williams - who is like a second mother to me - and my Godmother Alice Benjamin have been solid rocks of support. Your kind words of inspiration, cards of blessings and phone calls provided a calming voice and reassured me during critical times that I was going to be just fine.

I owe an enormous debt of gratitude to those who gave me guidance and direction at various stages of my life. My siblings (nearly two dozen), nieces, nephews, cousins, adopted families, and godchildren have helped me to love and appreciate life and to grab hold of opportunities and make the best of them. I am especially grateful for my Forest Hill Baptist Church families and Pilgrim Way families who all played a vital part in my journey and made this destination worthwhile.

Despite a life filled with many challenges, I count it all joy!

Thank you, Retired Chief Freddie Lott, for hiring me at the Augusta Police Department. You gave me a chance to pursue a dream, a dream that has been richly lived. I am forever grateful to you.

Many thanks to Tony Walden and Richard Elim for seeing my potential and giving me an opportunity to work investigations. It was the catalyst to jumpstarting my career and helped me to see the bigger picture. I learned to be a servant leader, thanks to many of the skillsets you taught me.

My Godfather, Daniel J. Craig, is a very fine man to whom I owe so many thanks. Despite my impatient youthfulness, you taught me well. You helped me realize that one could not legislate morality, that family is truly invaluable, and that education is the key to ending societal ills. My time as an investigator with you was a tremendous learning experience. I learned to speak and think critically by watching you and so many other lawyers. Your dedication to your church helped me to become a better deacon and later Chairman of the Deacons at Forest Hill Baptist Church, a position I held for eight years. I knew if you could serve as district attorney, take care of your family, and ascend to a position as deacon in the Catholic Church simultaneously, that I could do similar work. I was always watching, even when you did not know it. I learned about capitalism and socialism from you, Nancy Johnson, and Barbara J. Smith while riding to the Atlanta Crime Lab, working on a murder case (early 90s).

To my friends who know of my imperfections, I am grateful for your guidance and support. Those reminders to always do what is right and to avoid those things, which may cause problems, are very much appreciated. Your encouragement and understanding have helped me to learn and grow. Geoffrey Fogus, while on break during a trial, taught me a great deal about Economics (more than I ever understood from my college professor). You taught me a lot about the Bible too.

A very special thanks to Lewis Blanchard, Grady Mobley, Ryan Mobley, Charles Green Sr., Bobby Williams Jr., Lucious Abrams, the late Ralph Dickey, Craig Carter, Judge Carl C. Brown, Pamela Lewis, Brenda Bell Johnson, Elizabeth Billips, Annette Ports, Lee David Woods, James "Jim" Gordon, Leroy Robinson and all my beautiful coworkers for being wonderful people to be around and to learn and grow with. You have helped me more than I can ever express to you.

I am also immensely grateful to my friends and attorneys, Joe Neal Jr., and Igna N. Hicks. Both of you believed in me when I needed you most. Your legal minds are indescribable, and your genuine pursuit of justice is impeccable.

Writing a book about your life is a surreal process. I am forever indebted to Ty Hager for his editorial help, keen insight, and ongoing support in bringing my stories to life. It is because of his efforts and encouragement that I have a legacy to pass on to my family where one did not exist before.

To all the individuals I have had the opportunity to lead, be led by, or watch their leadership from afar, I want to say thank you for being the inspiration and foundation for my success. Without the experiences and support from my peers and friends like Sheriff John Wilcher and Dean Crisp, this book would not exist. You have given me the opportunity to lead a great group of individuals.

Thank you to our leadership team at the Burke County Sherriff's Office.

I want to thank EVERYONE who ever said anything positive to me or taught me something. I heard it all, and it meant something. My schoolteachers and employers alike were the best!

I want to thank God most of all, because without Him I wouldn't be able to do any of this.

Alfonzo Williams, May 2020

Sheriff Alfonzo's Famous POUND CAKE

Use quality ingredients and lots of love for the best results. White Lily Plain flour is preferred. Sifting flour results in a fluffier cake. So I would suggest a few sifts.

Ingredients:
4 sticks Salted Butter
4 Cups plain all-purpose flour
6 Room temperature eggs
3 Cups white granulated sugar
¾ Cups whole milk
1 tablespoon Vanilla Extract
1 teaspoon Lemon Extract

Directions:
Beat softened butter until smooth. Add sugar to butter and cream until fluffy. Add eggs 1 at a time, beating well between each egg. Add 1 cup of sifted flour and half of milk, mix well. Add remainder of flour and milk, mix well. Add Vanilla and Lemon extract. Pour batter into a prepared greased (with Crisco solid) and floured 10 in., 14 cup fluted cake pan. Bake 1 hour 45 minutes at 300 degrees

4 sticks	Salted Butter
3 C	Sugar
6	Eggs
4 C	Plain Flour (all-purpose) sifted
¾ C	Whole Milk
1 Tbs	Vanilla Extract
1 tsp	Lemon Extract

Made in the USA
Columbia, SC
28 November 2021